UNIVERSITY SUCCESS

THE
CHRISTIAN
PERSPECTIVE

DR. JOSEPHINE SHANGKUAN ONG

KENDALL/HUNT PUBLISHING COMPANY
4050 Westmark Drive   Dubuque, Iowa 52002

Copyright © 1996 by Josephine Shangkuan Ong

ISBN 0-7872-2788-9

Printed in the United States of America
10 9 8 7

Dedication

This book is dedicated to
my parents, Mr. and Mrs. Shih Chang Shangkuan
my husband, Dr. DeWitt Ong
my children, Natalie, Mimi, Didi, Justin, and Jordan.
They show me how to be a winner.

Acknowledgments

My thanks to all who worked on the preparation of this book:
Carla Bruce provided the editing and technical assistance.
James Chang provided the illustrations.
Dr. Dennis Ichiyama suggested the cover design.

The following people contributed materials for the various topics:

Rev. Richard Hendrix (Formula for Success)
Dr. Cathy Stafford (Learning Styles)
Jean Kiser (Health and Fitness)
Dr. Tom Hancock (Effective Communication)
Ted Malone (Managing Your Finances at College)
Dr. James Witherspoon (Choosing a Career and Major)
Gary Kilduff (Balancing Life's Demands)

Finally, thanks to Don Thoren, Dr. Larry Barron, and Dr. Leslie Dodrill
for the writing of their respective chapters.

Contents

Foreword

It is a privilege for me to be able to recommend *University Success, the Christian Perspective*. Dr. Ong has presented these materials with great success on our campus, and I believe this information provided our students with the strongest orientation possible to help them make the very best of their college experience.

Dr. Ong's strong background in teaching and personal experience is expressed in these materials, and I think this book will be very helpful, encouraging, and productive to all those using it.

Dr. Bill Williams, President, Grand Canyon University

It has been a delightful experience to serve as a resource faculty person for Dr. Josephine Ong in her course called "University Success." Dr. Ong has designed a dynamic course for new students to our University which exposes them not only to tips on successful academic experience, but to a vibrant and stimulating social environment.

I receive numerous letters from students who have completed the University Success class extolling its positive impact on their university careers, enhancing not only their classroom performance, but also giving them confidence in their interpersonal relationships with fellow students and faculty.

Dr. Ong's love of the Lord and commitment to helping students succeed makes her course a very popular selection for Grand Canyon University students.

Dr. Martha Taylor Thomas, Provost,
Vice President for External Affairs, Grand Canyon University

Dr. Josephine Ong has been a dynamic force on the campus of Grand Canyon University for some seven years now in her primary role of teaching chemistry to undergraduate students. Because of her rapport with students and her demonstrated ability to communicate with students, she seemed a logical choice to develop and carry out a new course envisioned as a way to smooth the transition from one way of life (high school, junior college, or work) to another (the private, four-year, Christian university) In addition, she had successfully taught a short course called "The Winning Edge" in our January Term for several years. This course sought to expose students to strategies and techniques for being a "success" in all areas of their lives: spiritual, emotional, social, intellectual and physical. The class is very popular with, and much appreciated by, students.

The book you are about to read is the result of this background combined with four semesters of solid experience in actually developing and coordinating this new course which came to be called "University Success." It definitely fills a gap in the literature available as a text for a course like this in a Christian college or university. Dr. Ong's radiant Christian spirit will shine through to you on every page and her hard-won insights and information will be helpful to students embarking on an educational experience at a Christian institution. I think you will enjoy what you read here!

Charles Maxson, Ph.D. Vice President for Academic Affairs, Grand Canyon University

Most new students, at some time or another, sense that college is confusing and frustrating, and that's pretty normal. Do you feel like that, and do you wonder if there is any real help available? Worry no more. Dr. Ong's book is designed with you in mind; it will help you find and stay on a solid path to college success.

This tool will get you started right for a successful college career. Glance over the chapters. Each gives clear, easy to follow directions for specific problem areas. Practical! The whole book provides you practical, down-to-earth guidance and instruction—and all from a Christian perspective.

Do three things. Carefully study each chapter as assigned. Do the discussion questions and exercises. Apply what you learn to all your college studies. And then let the Master Teacher be your ultimate teacher.

Dr. D.C. Martin, Chairman of Christian Studies, Grand Canyon University

UNIVERSITY
SUCCESS

A university is truly an exciting place; yet, for new students, it can be an overwhelming and a confusing place. For entering freshmen, you will be wading into uncharted waters, trying to keep your head above a sea of classes, prerequisites, majors, minors, a new found sense of freedom, new independence, and tremendous responsibilities.

For returning adults, the problems inherent in being a new student are magnified because college is usually not your only priority. You may have to juggle jobs, a spouse, children, commuting to and from other responsibilities in your community. Time management becomes a colossal undertaking. Some of you may have been away from formal education for a while, and may find your study skills, such as math computations, computer training, and test taking skills a bit rusty. You may be anxious about competing with younger students.

For transfer students, there are added concerns for details such as the number of credits that can be properly transferred, the pressure of choosing an appropriate major, guidance for applicable careers, and of being able to "fit in" a seemingly well-established environment where everyone seems to know exactly what they are doing.

Regardless of whether you are a traditional freshman or a returning adult, whether you are eighteen or thirty, the question of "Will I succeed?" is probably foremost in your mind. The first semester in college is crucial to you as a barometer of your potential success. Wouldn't it be wonderful if you were given a ticket that would enhance your success from the moment you set foot on the college campus?

At Grand Canyon University, I have designed a program called "University Success" to assist the new students and to enhance their success in college. University Success is a program designed to meet the needs of new students, transfer students, and returning adults. It is a course that addresses the four critical areas for student success: academic skills, life-management skills, campus and community awareness, personal and spiritual growth. The topics covered include: Formula for Success, Time Management, Learning Styles, Making the Grade, Making Friends, Health and Fitness, Effective Communication, Choosing a Career and a Major, Managing Your Finances, Keeping Faith, and Balancing Life's Demands.

Students in the program register for a one graded credit hour with the class meeting once a week for seminars, discussions, and group activities. Students are also linked with mentors and peer counselors who assist them with academic and personal issues, and even take them out to lunch from time to time.

Research shows that students who took a college success course completed more semester credits, earned a higher GPA, and had a lower drop-out rate than those who did not take such a course. The benefits are numerous: academic, career, and life goals are in focus; studying is more productive; grades improve; support groups are established; study skills are enhanced; school is more enjoyable, and employability is enhanced.

Students had this to say about "University Success."

"I learned more useful information in this class than any class I took. What I learned in 'University Success' is all practical information that I can use the rest of my life."

"I have learned countless things throughout this semester, and I would suggest that any student attending college take such a course."

This book is the outcome of the University Success Program. I have chosen twelve of the most pertinent and helpful topics presented in the program to be included in this book. The purpose is to help all new students everywhere, including traditional freshmen, transfer students, and returning adults during the critical first semester of their college career. The book is unique in the sense that *University Success* is viewed from the Christian perspective and fortified with values that are centered in Jesus Christ.

Read on and achieve UNIVERSITY SUCCESS!

Dr. Josephine S. Ong

Formula for Success

$$\text{Success} = (\text{Su})c^2 es^2 = \sum_{1}^{5} n$$

such that:

1 = read widely.
2 = choose your friends wisely.
3 = set specific goals.
4 = become a person of inte...
5 = CENTER YOUR LIFE ON
    JESUS CHRIST.

1

Formula for Success

*Certain proven ingredients contribute to your success;
not only your success in college, but throughout your life.*

A formula for success could be different things for different people. Certainly there is no one single formula for success. However, there are certain proven ingredients that will contribute to your success. Five of these ingredients will be explored in this chapter.

These five things are neither the beginning nor the end of success. Many other things contribute to success. But these might be five small stones to help you build the path toward success in your life.

You have already taken a step in that path to success by enrolling in college. Whether you are a freshman, transfer student, or incoming student of any description, these five ingredients can help you in your university career. But they can do more. These ingredients can be building blocks that help you throughout the rest of your life. Some of the patterns you set now are absolutely essential patterns for your future.

I. READ WIDELY

To read widely, you must first read well. Are you one of those students who read well and enjoy reading? You have a head start. But you might want to take a rapid reading course and learn to read faster and understand more. Excellent reading courses are available. Perhaps your school offers one; ask your professors or counselors.

Do you hate to read, consider it hard work, and it's what you dread most about college? If you don't have a good reading background, if you aren't prepared for all the reading you will have to do in college, then your first step should be to seek help.

The only thing worse than having a reading problem is having a reading problem and not doing anything about it. Don't be embarrassed to go to your faculty adviser or mentor, or to some other person you trust, and say, "I'm having trouble with reading. I can't read that fast. I can't understand some of what I'm reading. I need help."

Are you one of those who save all of the reading for the last night of the quarter or semester? That habit will cripple you for the rest of your life in terms of growing and learning, of being productive and successful. New reading habits are a must.

Learn to read.
Learn to love to read.

Suggested reading

To be successful in this information age, you must read. In 1990 more than fifty thousand new titles were published in the United States alone. How many of those books did you read? Of course no one expects you to read thousands, or even hundreds. But you must read widely if you're going to stay alert and stay up on the information explosion in your generation. Your generation, more than any other in history, must be readers.

Read a daily newspaper. Read more than the sports page, the department store ads, or the want ads. Start with the first section and read the news.

A good habit to develop is to begin the day with a daily newspaper. Of course, many Christians prefer to read the Bible the first thing in the morning. If you prefer to start with the Bible, that's fine. But read the newspaper sometime during the day and find out what's going on in the world.

Read a news magazine every week. Read *Time, Newsweek, US News and World Report.* Read something that tells you what's going on in the world. You may not read all the articles in depth. You may just scan some of them. But stay up with what's going on in the world.

Read books for growth. Read books that relate to your field of study and special interests. If you have already declared a major, pay attention to what is being published in that field. Your professors can be a great help with that. They will give you a reading list far in excess of what you are actually able to read.

Continue to read books for growth after you get out of college. Don't develop an attitude that says, "I've read my last textbook. I've read the last thing on this subject!"

- ✔ Keep reading
- ✔ Keep studying
- ✔ Keep growing

Read for spiritual growth. Read both Christian classics and contemporary works. If you've never read anything by C. S. Lewis, go to the library, dig out the card catalog and find the dozen or more titles that he's written: *Mere Christianity, Surprised by Joy, Problem of Pain,* and others. Go to a Christian bookstore and browse through the variety of books now available.

The person who does not read is not substantially better off than the person who cannot read.

Read for fun. Reading is fun and you ought to enjoy reading. Read some novels. Even if you only read a few pages at a time, it's good to keep a novel going all the time. Read entertaining and fun books, like Erma Bombeck's, *It's Time to Go Home When You Start to Look Like Your Passbook Photo.* Reading for fun will increase your reading speed and comprehension.

The biggest obstacle to reading. It's not poor reading skills; or limited reading comprehension; or that you can't find exciting, entertaining material. The biggest obstacle to reading is television.

Turn off the television. Or better still, if you have one in your room, get rid of it until after you graduate from college. You will not miss a thing and life will go on. Four years from now, when you graduate, you can just pick up with whatever it is you're used to watching.

The talk show hosts will still be talking about the same things four years from now.

Television is a passive medium; it keeps you from thinking, from responding, from interacting. Read. It's more fun. It engages your mind. Sometime every week turn off the TV and read instead.

One professor said, "You'll be the same person four years from now when you graduate from college, except for two things: the people with whom you associate and the books you read. "

II . CHOOSE YOUR FRIENDS WISELY

When you were a child the strongest influence in your life was your parents. In your teen years, particularly in high school, the influence of your friends became greater. Now that you are in college, your parents will no longer be the most influential people in your life; now it will be the people you freely choose to be your friends. For the next few years, your attitudes, behavior, and values will be influenced and shaped more by your friends than by any other single influence.

This is true even though you are a Christian, even though you attend church, pray, and read the Bible. Yes, those things do influence and shape your life. But the people you choose to associate with also have a tremendous influence on who you are and who you will become. Choose them wisely.

> *The Bible says that bad company corrupts good morals.*

Missionary dating. Occasionally someone will say, "I'm choosing people for friends that I can influence for good." Usually it works the other way. Missionary dating rarely works.

A girl may say, "I know this guy is a loser, but I'm going to win him to Christ. It would be so great if he believed in Jesus. And I'm just the person to win him to the Lord." Or the fellow says, "I know she doesn't love God. She doesn't know Him at all. But I'm going to influence her to know Christ." Maybe. But most often the opposite happens.

The downward pull is always the path of least resistance; we tend to sink to a lower level almost unconsciously. For example, if children of different ages—say, four through nine—are put together in a room and left without supervision to play with toys, books or games, you'll find that in a short time the children are all playing at the four-year-old level. It just happens that way.

> *Choose friends carefully. Their behavior, beliefs and values will rub off on you.*

III . SET SPECIFIC GOALS

If you were asked to list several goals for your life, what would they be? While it isn't possible or even necessary to have every area of your life programmed and planned, you do need some goals.

Most of us don't have trouble achieving the goals we set for ourselves. We only have trouble setting the goals in the first place.

Goals are different from wishes. You may wish for a red Ferrari, but have no plans to acquire one. You may wish you could play basketball like Michael Jordan, but it's not really a goal in your life. Wishes are the things you talk and dream about, but they are not things you're willing to work for.

Have goals in all areas of your life. What kind of career would you like to have? Do you intend to get married and have children? Where do you plan to live? What kind of family do you want to raise? How do you want to spend your leisure time? What recreational activities and hobbies would you like to spend time, energy and money on? What about your spiritual life? Would you like to understand more about the Bible? Do you desire to develop a more satisfying personal devotional time? Set goals in those areas. Set academic goals. Why are you in college? What are you hoping to do? Is a Bachelor's Degree the terminal degree for you? Will you pursue a Master's Degree? Will you go on with your Doctoral studies? Do you plan on post-doctoral work? Set those goals before you. Be specific, then plan accordingly.

Goals don't have to be grand and lofty. In fact, many ought to be bite-sized, incremental goals that lead to a larger accomplishment. Perhaps your long term objective is to earn a Bachelor's Degree, be on the Dean's List, and graduate with honors from this university. It will take many small goals along the way to accomplish those larger goals.

A goal says:
I'm aiming at a specific
target. I'm willing to work for it.
I will take the necessary steps
to achieve it.
I will move forward,
in a planned progression
toward the accomplishment
of that goal.

A shorter term objective toward that larger objective could be to get all A's and B's this semester. Then to achieve that goal, you will have to do certain things:

✔ Show up for class.

✔ Do the assigned reading.

✔ Turn assignments in on time.

✔ Do the term papers.

To achieve these small goals, you will probably have to do some homework every night rather than waiting and doing three all-nighters in a row at the end of the semester. Setting intermediate and incremental goals is essential.

Goals should be specific. Make your goals specific enough to be remembered. You should be able to say to yourself and to others, "I'm a person on a mission. I know where I'm going. I know what I want to achieve."

Then as you consider behavior and values, as you choose ways to spend your time, you can ask yourself: Does this fit? Do I really want to give my time and energy to this? Or am I feeling pressured to do it by peers or by someone who doesn't share my values and my goals?

Goals should be challenging. Are you doing anything in your life that makes you stretch? Are you doing anything that's harder than you think you're able to do? Choose goals that require you to stretch, that make you reach out further than you thought you could.

One pastor told of setting a goal to do something that for him was frightening, something that made him stretch out into another area. He was not a soloist, but he set a goal to sing a solo in church. He laughed as he told this story and said people in church came to him afterwards and said, "Please don't set that goal again."

Every year it's good to set a goal that will make you stretch further than you thought you could. If you're scared of computers, take a basic computer science course. Stretch. If you love music, but you're not a music major, take a music class, learn some theory, or take a voice performance class. Try something new.

Make many goals that all stretch toward a life objective. Set some spiritual, emotional, personal, financial, career and relationship goals so that you know where you're going.

> *Goals will make a path for your life.*

Hindrances. Sometimes you will encounter bumps and barricades along the path you have chosen, and they will take you off on unplanned side paths. It's good to remain open and flexible at such times. Never be so rigid that you do not leave room for God to add to, broaden, or stretch your goals.

The writer of Proverbs said, "We make our plans, but the outcome is in God's *hands*."

IV. BECOME A PERSON OF INTEGRITY

To be truly successful in any area of life, you must be a person of integrity. Whatever you choose to be—whether it's a minister, a nurse, a doctor, a lawyer, an accountant, a truck driver, a school teacher, a professor, a researcher, a politician, or a statesman—you must first be a person of integrity.

Integrity has to do with who you are on the inside, with who you are when the lights go off. C. S. Lewis once said that the fact that there are rats in your cellar is not so surprising. Who you are, though, is demonstrated when suddenly you burst into the cellar with no warning and no lights on and the rats are caught.

It's easy to put on a face, to act right in public, to do the proper things in school, at church and at home. But who you really are is who you are when the lights go out. Who you are is really evident only to you and God when you're absolutely alone.

The test of your personal integrity is who you are and what you are like when no one is watching.

Integrity is at risk today

Simple truth-telling. Be truthful through and through. Be truthful in relationships with your friends, your peers, your employer, or those whom you supervise. In all relationships let truth be the only method of communication.

If you are not an absolute rigid truth-teller, you will find that dishonesty and lies eventually spill out of the little area where you think they are confined and into all the areas of your life. Don't give dishonesty a foothold anywhere in your life. Always tell the truth.

Yes, there are people who will say that there are times and situations when telling the truth is not the loving thing to do. Yet the Bible always holds up the standard of truth.

The Apostle Paul said to speak the truth in love:

> *"...We will lovingly follow the truth at all times—speaking truly, dealing truly, living truly—and so become more and more in every way like Christ...."*
> Ephesians 4:15 (TLB)

How you speak the truth is just as important as speaking it. This does not mean that you must express your opinion on every topic that arises; but if a response is necessary on your part, let your words be truth.

Tell the truth always, for your sake; then when you go to sleep at night you don't have to keep track of what you told who. It is so peaceful to be able to fall asleep at night knowing there's nothing to be found out.

A man who had been caught in a series of perversions in his business life asked a minister this question: "Do you have skeletons in your life? Are there things hidden away that you hope people never find out about?" The minister replied that he supposed he had lived a really dull life because he couldn't think of a thing. That man had made a practice of being truthful.

Live out your values. Many Christians are at terrible risk today of saying one thing and living something else. If you say "Jesus is Lord of my life," make sure it's not just something you sing on Sundays. Be absolutely certain that your lifestyle demonstrates what you believe.

---

*Decide ahead of time
what your values are
and what your choices will be.*

If Jesus is truly Lord of your life you will have concern for the poor, compassion for people who are broken and hurting, and a sense of obligation that the gospel inside of you spill out onto the destitute people who are all around us.

In baseball it's essential to know what to do if the ball is hit to you. Baseball players are taught what plays to make in a variety of situations. Because they know ahead of time what they should do, they make the correct play when the ball is hit to them.

Plan ahead how you will respond in certain situations that might come up. Decide now in the bright lights of the classroom the choices you will make sexually when the lights go out. Waiting until you are faced with that choice increases your chances of making the wrong one. If you wait until your hormones are running your life, you won't make an informed choice. You won't make a competent choice. You won't make a spiritually motivated choice. You won't even make a rational and intelligent choice. You'll make a hormonal choice.

The sad commentary of those who allow their hormones to make the choice goes something like this: But I didn't intend for it to happen. I didn't plan it. I just got carried away before I knew what I was doing.

✔ Have a plan.

✔ Make your choice beforehand.

✔ Take charge of your life.

You are not just a bundle of hormones. You are so much more. You are a whole person: a spirit, a mind, a will, and a set of emotions.

A lady in a very successful position with a large international company was asked by her employer to falsify government records that would mean millions of dollars for the company. She considered her options, "If I don't sign, I lose my job. But if I do sign, I've broken the law. I've broken my own conscience." She refused to sign. She valued integrity, and had already made a decision to do the right thing.

If you wait until you're under fire, you might make the wrong choice. If you want to be a person of integrity, then decide now what choices you will make and how you will live.

V. CENTER YOUR LIFE ON JESUS CHRIST

You will be off center if Jesus Christ is not the center point for your life. The word *eccentric* means off center, off balance. If you have studied centrifugal force, you know that anything that is even slightly off center will wobble.

If your life is centered around anything or anyone other than Jesus Christ, you are eccentric, off center, out of balance, and your life will wobble.

> *You don't have to wobble through life. You can go through life orbiting smoothly if your center is Jesus Christ.*

A career cannot be the center of your life. Financial security, having a fine home and a good car, will not function well at the center of your life. There's nothing wrong with those things; they are fine things for out there on the edge.

Being a four sport letter athlete is not worth being the center of your life. Getting married to the most beautiful girl at school, or the smartest, most handsome guy at school cannot be the center of your life. Having wonderful children who grow up and go to Sunday School and love Jesus cannot be the center of your life.

Only one person, one thing, one reality in this universe qualifies to be the center of your life—and that is Jesus Christ. Make Him the center of your life.

- ✔ No other relationship will satisfy as deeply as a personal relationship with Christ.
- ✔ No other goal will motivate as well.
- ✔ No other ambition or relationship will satisfy you for the years and years of your life.

Wouldn't you like to live out your life on center without wobbling? Make Jesus Christ the center of your life and you'll be able to do that for now and for all of eternity.

To make Jesus the center of your life requires time.

Spend time reading the Bible. Of all the books you read, spend time in that Book.

> *"...Meditate on the Word of God so that you may be careful to do everything written in it. Then you will be prosperous and successful."*
> Joshua 1:8 (NIV)

Spend time in prayer. Talk to God and learn to listen to His still small voice within.

Spend time serving Jesus. If you don't have a place where you're giving away a part of yourself, find a place. Coach Little League. Teach Sunday School in your church. Work with the Junior Choir. Sing a solo. Join the adult choir. Join the college choir. You might want to work with international students who need to learn English as a second language. Or work with poor students in your neighborhood who need a tutor after school.

Do something to give away part of yourself. That is centering on Jesus.

Jesus gave Himself away—and not just a part. He gave all of Himself away—His whole life—everything.

Centering your life on Jesus will help you in the first four points in your formula for success. Centering your life on Jesus will enhance everything you do. The Apostle Paul put it this way in Acts 17:28, "...in Him we live and move and have our being...."

Chapter One

Discussion Questions and Exercises

1. Why do you think reading is so important in the "Information Age" in which we live?

   _____

   _____

   _____

   _____

   _____

   List three benefits of reading:

   a. _____

   b. _____

   c. _____

2. Write the name of a book you plan to read this coming week.

   _____

   List two books you would like to read this semester.

   _____

   _____

3. Learn to use the Internet. Go to the library, a friend's house, or use your own computer and extract an article on a topic of your choice from the Internet. Write the title of the article and the name of the author.

   _____

4. Respond (from personal experience, if possible) to the biblical statement, "Bad company corrupts good morals."

_____

_____

_____

_____

_____

_____

5. List five attitudes, behaviors, or moral values you look for in a friend.

a. _____

b. _____

c. _____

d. _____

e. _____

6. Practice writing positive, measurable, and realistic goals.

Write five short term goals for this semester.

a. _____

b. _____

c. _____

d. _____

e. _____

Write two long term goals for your college education.

a. _____

b. _____

Make a copy of these goals and put it in your purse or wallet. Refer to it at least once a day.

7. Name some areas where personal integrity is essential, yet is under attack today. What areas as a person, a Christian, a student, a man or woman present challenges to your integrity today?

a. _____

b. _____

c. _____

8. What are some specific evidences of you centering your life on Jesus Christ?

a. _____

b. _____

c. _____

9. What values, choices and decisions will be affected when you make Jesus Christ the Lord of your life?

a. _____

b. _____

c. _____

Checklist for Services and Assistance

- ☐ I want help in deciding what I should study in college.
- ☐ I want help in deciding what occupation to pursue.
- ☐ I want to improve my grades.
- ☐ I feel very lonely.
- ☐ I need financial assistance.

- ☐ I am very anxious when I take tests.
- ☐ I need a part time job.
- ☐ I have been out of school for years, and I feel lost.
- ☐ I have a serious problem with my parents or spouse.
- ☐ Others

List your concerns:

a. _____

b. _____

c. _____

d. _____

A counselor at your university can help you with your problems or tell you where you can find help.

♥ ♥ ♥

Scripture and Prayer

For I know the plans I have for you, says the Lord. They are plans for good and not for evil, to give you a future and a hope. Jeremiah 29:11 TLB

Heavenly Father,

I thank you for all the people—family, friends, teachers, pastors—who have influenced my life for good. I thank you for the encouragement, guidance, support, and provision they have given me over the years.

Now, as I begin this new and exciting time of my life as a college student, I ask you to help me build wisely upon this good foundation that others have laid. Help me to make intelligent decisions that will contribute to my success in college. Help me each day to center my life on Jesus Christ. And thank you that not only do you want me to have success in life, but you have planned many, many good things for me.

amen

Time Management

The Juggling Act

2

Time Management

*Time management is a plan for the way you live—
it is managing your time well.*

Time management is not a new concept. The Bible speaks of it, and so did many successful men and women of the past.

> *"There is a time for everything and a season for every activity under heaven."* Ecclesiastes 3:1

> *"Be very careful then of how you live - not as unwise, but as wise, making the most of every opportunity."* Ephesians 5:15, 16

> *"Dost thou love life? Then do not squander time, for that is the stuff that life is made of."* Benjamin Franklin

> *"Yesterday is already a dream, and tomorrow only a vision; but today well lived, makes every yesterday a dream of happiness, and every tomorrow a vision of hope."* Anonymous

Personal Example

When people sometimes ask me how I can do so many things, I reply, "By the grace of God and time management."

I live by the principles I am sharing in this chapter. They work for me, and I know they will work for you. Without time management I could not do all the things that are important to me.

At Grand Canyon University, I am the Director of the University Success Program and I am a chemistry professor—that's my career. A few years ago I was a full-time student at Arizona State University working on my doctorate degree. I'm a wife and a mother of five very active children.

At the church, I direct the choir and play the organ. I'm a Sunday School teacher and Youth Counselor.

In the community, I'm a member of the Maricopa County Board of Supervisors—The Citizen Bond Committee.

Socially, I'm a member of several professional associations: The American Chemical Society, and The Chinese American Professional Association. In addition, I come from a large family, and we get together for birthdays, reunions and special occasions.

As a professional in education, I know the importance of time management. As students, you are also professionals. When you attend college you become professional students; you make a com-

mitment for an extended period— probably four years of your lives. Therefore, you need to organize your time wisely.

I. SET PRIORITIES

The first step in time management is setting priorities. As a new university student, your first priority should be planning your first semester. To do that you will need the following:

- ✔ A master's schedule, which includes the major events for the semester, including midterms and final examinations. Fill in the important events, then plan other things around them.

- ✔ A course syllabus, which tells you the content of the course and the chapters that will be covered.

- ✔ A course schedule of classes you have signed up to take.

- ✔ A student calendar where each day you can write down your class assignments. Include a column headed "my stuff" for your social and recreational activities. When you work hard, you should also play hard.

**A Time Organizer Schedule
is provided for you
at the end of this chapter.**

---

1. Schedule in committed times

For example, on Thursday from 10:30 to 11:45 you may be committed to the Freshman Seminar. Monday, Wednesday and Friday mornings from 8:40 to 9:30, you are committed to Chemistry 101. You can't change those, so fill them in first.

2. Color-code individual class hours

You might use red for math, blue for English, etc. For every hour class that you take, expect two hours preparation outside of class for your regular assignments. If you take a three-credit hour math class, set aside at least six hours study time. Color-code your study block time to correspond with your class time.

If you are a working student, or a mother with children at home, finding a solid block of hours for study could be impossible. What do you do then?

3. Steal time during the day

Steal the fifteen minutes you wait for the bus, the half-hour you wait for the laundry to dry, the half-hour you wait for children at piano lessons. Steal those times and study for your classes. You can even study while you're sunbathing by the pool. Learn to steal time during the day.

4. Have a daily schedule

Use a pocket size appointment book, and write a "to do" list for each day.

Stick-on notes are also helpful. I use them for my daily driving schedule. I write down where I need to go and what time I need to be there, or when and where I should pick up my children. The stick-ons go on the dashboard of my car, and I pull them off one by one as I do them.

Here's an example of one of my typical daily "to do" lists.

Speak in University Success Class
Pick up the blinds at the store
Meet the assistants at 10 o'clock
Check the tape recorder
Check the camera
Deliver tape to transcriber
Meet Directors of Resource Center
Prepare lectures for chemistry
Fix dinner
Return sandwich maker to store
Go to the twins' volleyball game
Redo nails

After making my "to do" list, I prioritize it. Some things will be A, some B, some C, maybe even a D.

For example, I put an A beside speaking in the University Success Class and preparing class lectures. Meeting with the Director of Resource Center might be a B. Fix dinner, a C (we can call Kentucky Fried Chicken). Redo nails, maybe a C or D (I can just paint over them). Return the sandwich maker might even be an F (I could do that another day).

Do the A items first each day, then tackle the B items. If you can't do C and D, don't worry about them. By doing the A and B items, you have accomplished the most important things.

Mark off each task as you finish.
This gives you a sense
of accomplishment.

II. SET GOALS

The second step in time management is setting goals. Set short-term and long-term goals. Write down your goals for the first semester, for one year, and then for four years.

What do you want to accomplish in school this year? Is your goal to get all A's? or A's and B's this first semester? Would you like to have a 3.75 GPA at the end of the year? Do you plan to graduate in four years?

Then think about long term goals: career, marriage, children, church, community, sports, or anything else that is important to you. Visualize yourself twenty years from now. What kind of life to you want to have?

To reach those goals, you will need to work hard and manage your time wisely. Here are some suggestions:

✔ **Set short-range goals.** Today, set a goal to make good use of your time. Determine to give your best effort to your lessons today. Then set a goal for the week, for the month, for six months.

✔ **Set realistic goals.** In the beginning set goals that are easy to accomplish, so you do not become disappointed. Break down your goals to a series of absurdly easy steps so that you can accomplish them.

✔ **Set incremental goals** that you can accomplish as part of your big objective.

✔ **Get group reinforcement.** A support group can help you achieve your goals.

✔ **Ceremonialize your achievement.** Give yourself a certificate, a reward, a new outfit, or even a short trip if you can afford it.

To illustrate these five points, let's see how they would work if your goal was to lose twenty pounds.

First, set short range goals. Today you will skip one dessert out of the three you normally eat. For the first week, your goal is to lose just one pound—that's achievable. In one month you will lose one inch from your waistline. In six months you will lose the twenty pounds.

Set realistic goals that are easy to accomplish. Let's say you decide to skip a dessert of three scoops of ice cream, but it's hard to give up ice cream for right now. You could just knock it down from three scoops to two scoops and skip the whipped cream and cherries. You can do that just for today; you can take that first step that puts you on the way to success.

Set incremental goals. Keep a record of your weight loss each week. One pound a week, step by step. Before you know it, you will have lost the twenty pounds.

Get group reinforcement. Join an aerobics class or a support group of people who have similar goals.

Ceremonialize your achievement. Buy a new outfit. Hang it on your refrigerator door to remind you that in six months you'll be a size five, down from a size twelve.

Let's apply these five steps to school work. Your goal is to have an excellent term paper.

Start now with a short-range goal. The first week you will go to the library and read something on this topic, and you will write just one paragraph. Your goal for the month could be to have several pages finished. By the end of the semester, you will have a wonderful term paper.

Get group reinforcement by joining a study group. Then at the end of the semester, go out together for a pizza or something. Ceremonialize your achievement when you reach your goals.

Be flexible. Circumstances can change. Unpredictable events can happen. For example, during the Persian Gulf War, many people had to leave school and work to be a part of Desert Storm.

Delegate. This is a key to successfully achieving your goals. One of my goals is to keep my house clean while I juggle all the other activities in my life. I delegated one of my daughters to be the Director of Laundry and another to be the Director of Dishes. My son is the Director of Pets. The result is that my job of keeping the house clean is easier.

III. CULTIVATE GOOD ATTITUDES

A good attitude is a vital part of time management; a good attitude will give you the winning edge. What is the winning edge? It's easy to visualize in sports. In basketball the winning edge could be sinking that extra basket in the last second of play. In track and field, we would say that Carl Lewis has the winning edge because he's breaking the tape by two-hundredths of a second.

Examples of the winning edge are found in all walks of life:

Helen Keller was deaf and blind, yet she dedicated her life to others who were less fortunate.

Albert Einstein failed the college entry exam; his "SAT score" was low. Yet he went on to discover the theory of relativity.

Thomas Edison was labeled "unteachable." He only went through second grade. He became deaf when some experiments he was playing with in the backyard exploded. Yet he discovered the electrical bulb, and had more than one thousand original patents.

Lee Iacocca lost his job in his fifties. Yet he recovered from that and brought Chrysler Corporation out of bankruptcy.

Abraham Lincoln was born dirt-poor. He lost his sweetheart at age eighteen. He ran unsuccessfully for congressman and senator. Yet he became the best-loved President of the United States.

Winning attitudes enabled these people to rise above their circumstances and let them stay on top.

As you set your goals, remember that nothing is impossible with God. You can have the winning edge.

IV. DEVELOP WINNING QUALITIES

A book called *The Psychology of Winning* by Dennis Waitley mentions ten qualities that you should develop to succeed. We're only going to discuss one—positive self-discipline. This book states that self-discipline is the ability to practice within. The author says that winners are masters of the art of simulation. We see this in astronauts, championship athletes, stage performers, skilled surgeons, and professional executive salesmen. They practice quality techniques in their minds over and over.

> ***Self-discipline is an ability to practice within. It is mastering the art of simulation.***

Here's one way you can apply the principle of practicing within. Is your goal to graduate four years from now? Then imagine yourself walking up to the podium, reaching out and taking that diploma, hearing the cheers from your parents and friends. Do this over and over. See yourself graduating.

A winner is self-confidant. A winner's self-talk goes like this: Of course, I can do it. I have practiced it mentally a thousand times.

Let's say you want to get an A in Biology. Keep practicing and practicing—in your test and studying and simulating that A. Before you know it, you'll be holding a test paper marked A.

To practice within, to mentally simulate an activity, is common among successful people. Greg Luganis can perform those perfect dives, almost with his eyes closed, because he practiced so many times before.

The renowned pianist Van Cliburn sometimes sits with eyes closed on an airplane as he is flying to a concert. He practices inside his head, over and over, the pieces he will play that night.

I use this technique, while I'm driving, to practice directing the choir. The music is in my head, and I do keep both hands on the steering wheel. By Sunday I'm directing the choir perfectly because I have practiced many times before.

Practice will enable you to achieve your goals.

"Whoever loves discipline, loves knowledge." Proverbs 12:1

V. STUDY HELPS

1. Mystery Box

A useful study help is what I call "a mystery box." This is a box filled with items that can make study time easier and more profitable. I used a mystery box to get my doctorate degree. I use them to help my children study.

Make a mystery box that contains essential study items. You might include the following: five sharpened pencils; note cards for jotting down important items, important thoughts, or something you read; note pad and scratch paper; a kitchen timer is also essential.

Other items you should have in your mystery box: a calculator, a ruler; chemistry students would need a periodic table.

Write your goals on a note card—maybe even laminate it—and put it in the box. You might write: My goal is to graduate in four years. If you are a business major, you might have a goal to earn your first million by age thirty. Whatever your goal, this scripture is good to remember:

"Lazy hands make a man poor,
but diligent hands bring wealth."
Proverbs 10:4 (NIV)

2. Study in 30 minute segments

When you have everything set up to begin studying, set the timer for thirty minutes. Then work without distraction. Don't answer the phone or turn on the TV for that thirty minutes.

Why only thirty minutes? Because when you start studying, your concentration goes up. Beyond thirty minutes, your concentration starts going down. If you plan to study three hours, your level of concentration will go downhill during the last two hours unless you take breaks after each thirty minute segment.

After each thirty minutes of study, stop and give yourself a five minute break. Maybe have a nutritious snack: celery, banana, or high energy granola bar.

Now you're ready for the next thirty minutes. Set the timer and when it goes off, give yourself another break. That five minute break is enough to cause your concentration to go up again, so that you are making wise use of your time.

3. How to raise your grade

Here are some practical tips on how to raise your grade from C to B, and then from B to A.

✔ Do not miss class. Do not make excuses. Go to class every day.

✔ Do the reading assignment before coming to class. Even if you don't understand it, go ahead and faithfully read the assignment.

✔ Immediately after attending the lecture, read the notes that you have written. Then read that chapter again.

There's a Chinese saying that goes like this: *"I see and I forget. I hear and I remember. I do and I understand."*

The first time you read the assignment, you may forget. Then when you come to class and listen to the lecture, you remember. After that, you do the problem and you understand.

4. Study with a group

Two or three students can form a regular study group; what one person doesn't know, the other will.

5. Get help from your professors

Finally, be sure to use the professors' office hours. They are clearly listed outside their office doors. Your professors are there for you. They are your coaches. Make use of that time. Usually, people are shy about going to see their professors. They wait until they can't do the finals or some other important assignment. Then it's too late; start going at the beginning of the semester.

VI. CONSULT DAILY WITH GOD

Above all, consult with God daily. After you've set your goals and made plans for your life, remember that God is our source of wisdom.

Here's my favorite Bible verse:

"Trust in the Lord with all your heart, and lean not unto your own understanding. In all your ways, acknowledge Him and He will direct your path." Proverbs 3:23

Earlier we mentioned the importance of having a daily "to do" list. At the top of my "to do" list is to have a devotion each morning. I have a corner in my bedroom where each morning I talk with God. My husband and I lead very busy lives, but the first thing we do each day is talk to God. Sometimes the children join us.

We read the Bible together, tell God our problems, our plans, and ask Him to direct us.

"I have set the Lord always before me." Psalm 16:8

The Difference

I got up early one morning
And rushed right into the day;
I had so much to accomplish
That I didn't take time to pray.

Problems just tumbling about me
And heavier came each task;
"Why doesn't God help me?" I wondered.
He answered, "You didn't ask."

I wanted to see joy and beauty—
But the day toiled on, gray and bleak;
I wondered why God didn't show me,
He said, "But you didn't seek."

I tried to come into God's presence,
I used all my keys at the lock.
God gently and lovingly chided:
"My child, you didn't knock."

I woke up early this morning
And paused before entering the day;
I had so much to accomplish
That I had to take time to pray.
—*Author Unknown*

Chapter Two

Discussion Questions and Exercises

1. What are the "balls" that you are juggling now?

	Classes, job, family, etc.	Hours per week	New Priority	Hours to spend per week
a.				
b.				
c.				
d.				
e.				

2. Write down your short term and long term goals in the following areas:

	1 semester	1 year	4 years
School			
Career			
Church			
Family			
Community			

Others _____

_____

_____

_____

3. Name one bad habit that you wish to break TODAY and one good habit to replace it.

BAD HABIT _____

GOOD HABIT _____

4. Set the goals for your study time.
   List the courses you are taking, the grade you want for each course, and the number of hours per week you will need to study for each course to earn the grade you want.

Courses	Grades wanted	Hours needed to study
_____	_____	_____
_____	_____	_____
_____	_____	_____
_____	_____	_____
_____	_____	_____

5. Prepare a list of things you need to do next week. Prioritize the lists with A.B.C.D.E. Keep the list of "Things to Do Next Week" in your wallet or in your organizer and check it from time to time to remind yourself of your short term goals.

6. Make a calendar for the entire term using the following page as a guide.

   ■ Consult your school's catalog for the dates of holidays, vacation, final exams and other important dates.

   ■ Use the syllabus, outlines, and other materials your instructors give you to find the dates of tests and the dates term papers and other long term homework are due.

   ■ Use the school publications to find the dates of important athletic, church, and social events that you want to attend.

   ■ Use your personal records for the dates of weddings, birthdays, anniversaries and other important events that you observe with your friends and relatives

   ■ PRIORITIZE, PRIORITIZE, PRIORITIZE and make adjustments to do the things that matter.

♥ ♥ ♥

Scripture and Prayer

See then that you walk circumspectly, not as fools, but as wise, redeeming the time.... Ephesians 5:15,16

Heavenly Father,

You have given me the same amount of time you give to everyone—24 hours each day, 7 days each week, 52 weeks each year. Help me to use my time wisely. Help me to make plans and set priorities, to set goals and consistently work to achieve them.

Help me to cultivate good attitudes so that I don't waste time being bitter, resentful, or feeling sorry for myself. Help me to see myself as you see me—a person who can achieve and succeed.

Help me to use my allotted time for study to the best advantage, neither wasting it nor trying to do too much at one time. And especially remind me to take time for you each day, for that will help me accomplish everything else I have to do.

amen

Long Term Planner __/__/__ to __/__/__ Name _____

Week of	Mon.	Tues.	Wed.	Thurs.	Fri.	Sat.	Sun.
__/__							
__/__							
__/__							
__/__							
__/__							
__/__							
__/__							
__/__							
__/__							
__/__							
__/__							
__/__							
__/__							
__/__							
__/__							
__/__							
__/__							
__/__							
__/__							
__/__							
__/__							
__/__							
__/__							
__/__							

Time Organizer

	Monday__/__	Tuesday__/__	Wednesday__/__	Thursday__/__	Friday__/__
6:00					
7:00					
8:00					
9:00					
10:00					
11:00					
12:00					
1:00					
2:00					
3:00					
4:00					
5:00					
6:00					
7:00					
8:00					
9:00					
10:00					
11:00					
12:00					
1:00					
2:00					
3:00					
4:00					
5:00					

Chapter Three

Learning Styles

3

Learning Styles

People usually have a preference in how they like to learn.
We call that preference a learning style.

Would you like to cut down on study time? One way is to determine your most effective way to learn. We all have individual styles of learning. We have individual, characteristic ways that we process information. We also have individual ways of behaving in learning situations.

The Scriptures tell us that we are wonderfully, awesomely made; we are unique. We are made in God's image; we are created special. Part of this wonderful creation is the brain, with its ability to sort and to process information.

There are individual variations on how the brain processes information, depending on who we are and how we go about things. Our feelings about certain kinds of information also effect how we process it. Those feelings impact our behavior in learning situations.

For example, some people love mathematics and find it challenging. Others can't balance their checkbook and don't care. Likewise, many people thoroughly enjoy reading; they can just get lost in a book. Others read the headlines on the front page, and that's it. Some people enjoy the sciences; others are history buffs.

People who love chemistry will process information in that category differently from people who have no interest in chemistry. Therefore, the way people feel about certain subjects will impact how their brains work in processing information.

I. HOW DO YOU LEARN BEST?

The first essential in becoming a successful learner is to know yourself. Who are you as a learner? What do you know about yourself? How do you learn best? What is your style? How do you process information?

Three essentials to become a successful learner:

✔ Know Yourself.

✔ Apply Yourself.

✔ Believe in Yourself.

II. HOW INFORMATION GETS INTO THE BRAIN

Information comes through different channels of perception. We take in information by what we see, what we hear, what we touch, and what we do. Information comes through these channels: visual, auditory, tactile, and kinesthetic. After we take in information, we organize and process it.

People usually have one particular way in which it is easier for them to perceive—to take in information. They have a preference in how they like to learn. We call that preference a learning style.

A learning style is the manner in which the many different elements from the five basic stimuli affect our ability to absorb—and all important in college—to retain information. The five different stimuli through which perception comes and by which we begin to sort information are: environmental, emotional, sociological, physical, psychological. (See chart at the end of this chapter.)

Midterm and semester grade reports reflect how well students retain information as well as how well they are able to relate that information.

III. ENVIRONMENTAL

Certain factors and elements can impact our ability to process, absorb, and retain information. Environment, which includes sound, light, temperature, and design, is one of those factors. You need to determine what is most conducive to learning, and then try to study in that environment.

Sound. Are you easily distracted and need quiet? Or do you need some background sound or music?

Light. Do you need a bright light? Or do you prefer subdued lighting?

Temperature. If the room is too warm, do you get sleepy? Or if it's cold, does that distract you?

Design. Do you need to sit at a desk, with supplies neatly lined up: paper and pencils in place, dictionary and other reference books handy, rulers and calculators within reach? If a formal, orderly design works better for you, then it's worth the time and effort to set that up.

Other students study better in an informal room design. Do you like to sit on a pillow on the floor? Can you just plop down in the middle of everything? or push things to one side of the kitchen table? That's fine, if it works for you. The important thing is to know yourself—know your personal learning style.

What kind of environment works better for you in studying? If you could design the perfect place to study, what would it be like?

Rarely, however, is a perfect study environment possible. So you have to be realistic. Consider the place where you study, then determine how to help yourself by setting it up as nearly perfect as possible.

If you are easily distracted, studying in a dorm will not work well. A quiet corner in the library might be better. Make adjustments in the environment that will be more conducive to your learning style. The more you can do to help yourself, through creating a personalized study environment, the more you will cut down on study time. Determining your learning style will make study more streamlined and efficient.

IV. EMOTIONAL

Some emotional stimuli that affect us when we study are motivation, persistence, responsibility, and structure.

How motivated are you? That probably varies from class to class. Consider your current schedule; is it easier to study for some classes more than others?

When planning your schedule, it's good if you can to plan one or two classes that you enjoy and that motivate you.

How persistent are you? Can you start a task and see it through to the end, no matter what? Or do you let every distraction that comes along interrupt you?

How responsible are you? Do you still need your mother, or a mother-figure, to say, "Have you done your homework? Have you studied tonight?" You might not like for someone to oversee your study habits, but if you are honest you would have to admit you need that.

A big difference in high school and college is personal responsibility. College students have a tendency to look at their schedule, and seeing certain classes are Monday, Wednesday, and Friday, they consider the breaks as free time. But it isn't that way. The professors expect students to take responsibility and schedule appropriate study and preparation times.

4. How much structure do you need? Do you need step-by-step instructions to do well? Or are you the type who says,

"Just tell me what the bottom line is, and leave me alone"?

Some professors are extremely structured and give clear-cut expectations. Other professors have little structure. They might present the goals for the semester and ask the students to determine how they will reach those goals.

Many students cannot handle an unstructured class, but others thrive in that atmosphere. Determine what works for you. And when you can, choose classes that give you an advantage because they fit your learning style.

To do well in your classes, there is no substitute for studying. You must allow time to study.

V. SOCIOLOGICAL

Learning strategies and styles are also affected by sociological stimuli. Do you study better with a group of people? Do you study better by yourself? Do you study better if you have one other person to talk with and bounce ideas off?

Do you like small group assignments in your courses? How do you feel about the authority figure—the professor of the class? Do you need to be able to talk to the professor and ask questions? Are the professor's office hours important to you, because you like to stop by and check on assignments? Do you sometimes stay after class and talk to your professor to make sure you understand the next assignment?

Part of your style of learning might include the need to check in, to have somebody to help you, or to reassure you that your understanding is correct and that you are clear on what is expected of you.

Or are you the kind of person to whom the teacher could basically hand out the course syllabi and turn you loose and you could get it done? You prefer to handle it yourself. You like to run your own program, answer the questions, and explore the possibilities. The authority figure in the classroom is not essential to you.

Perhaps your learning style falls somewhere between the two extremes. You may need to check in with the professor occasionally, but it is also important for you to run your own program and make some decisions about assignments.

Consider how sociological stimuli impacts your learning style as you plan classes. Each professor has a different style. If you have the option of choosing a different professor for the same course, find out which professors run a course compatible with your most effective learning style.

VI. PHYSICAL

Another factor in learning is physical stimuli. Do you learn better by seeing? by hearing? by touching? by getting involved? Do you do well sitting for fifty minutes listening to a lecture? Does it help you to recall information when a professor puts up a visual picture or gives you a handout? Or do you do better in a class where you can get up and move and be involved?

Some classes—particularly the sciences, have a combination of lecture, where you listen and take in information, and also a lab where you put that information to work. Labs are a kinesthetic approach to learning.

What approach do you use on difficult test questions? How do you try to access the information? Do you close your eyes and try to see your notes? If so, you are probably a visual learner. Do you try to remember what the professor said? Then you are an auditory learner. Or does it help you to recall the lab you worked on? Then you are a kinesthetic learner; that's part of the physical perception.

After determining your learning strengths in this area, begin using that information to your advantage. For example, if you have determined that you are a visual learner, audio taping your classes would not be a help. Taking good, organized notes would be of the most help for a visual learner.

Taking detailed extensive notes in class distracts auditory learners. They miss the auditory information which is their strength. Auditory learners profit from audio taping the class and listening to it several times.

If you are the kinesthetic learner, one who needs hands-on involvement, what will work for you? Taking notes is beneficial, because it gets you involved. Talking about the information is also good. Find someone with whom you can work, talk to, interact and brainstorm. Ask someone to quiz you on the information. All of these will get you involved.

Whether your learning style is visual, auditory, tactile, or kinesthetic, go with your strengths. Use the methods that work for you.

Intake. Do you like to munch when you study? Some people work better if they "fuel it." Others do better if they just focus on the work and eat later. Munching distracts them.

Time of day. Are you bright-eyed and alert when you first get up? Or do you need a mid-morning nap? Are you still going strong at ten o'clock at night? All of this is part of your learning style.

When you are at your best—brain on and energy level high—is your ideal study time. However, that may not be realistic. For example, if you wake up at five a.m., raring to go, and you live in the dorms, that will not be popular with your room-mates.

Also, if the middle of the day is your best study time, you may have a job or other commitments that prevent you from studying at that time.

But try to design the most effective time to study. Take note of when your energy level is high. If you can study then, it is more efficient and you will need less study time.

Mobility. Does sitting for a long time make you uncomfortable? Do you need to get up periodically, walk around, and stretch during a study session? Taking a short break to get up and walk and stretch will boost your energy level, cause your blood to pump a little faster, and you will be more alert.

As you set up the physical aspect of studying, consider if you need to be someplace where you can move around. Or, if you're learning something tough, you might need to talk to yourself. That's part of mobility.

VII. PSYCHOLOGICAL

Analytical or global

Analytical learners need order: step one, step two, step three. They need information lined out so they can think about it sequentially. Analytical learners need to see all the details and steps before they can get the big picture. They have to understand all the whys and the details. Global learners do not want to be bothered with all the details. They want to know where the fine line is, without all the details to get there. They want to see the big picture.

A teacher whose learning approach is analytical will probably use many charts, giving step-by-step directions to the students. That will be fine for those students who are also analytical. But the global learners will not do as well with this style. Global learners need to see the overall picture first; then they can go back and consider each detail.

You need to be aware of your professors' teaching styles. Are some of them analytical and others global? How do they set up the course? And how does that compare with your learning style? All of this will make a difference in your approach to studying.

Right brain or left brain

Are you predominately a left brain thinker or are you a right brain thinker? A left brained thinker is language oriented, analytical, and sequential. A right brained thinker is abstract, spatially oriented, and language is not a preference.

Typically, we are a mixture of right and left brain preferences; but one will dominate and determine our most productive way to learn.

Do you need to be able to read it, write it, and talk about it? Or do you need to be able to think about the big spatial picture? Do you like to have a model or a chart and see how it all goes together? These differences are part of your cerebral preference.

Reflective or impulsive

Whether you are reflective or impulsive also impacts your style of learning. If you are reflective, you need to mull over, think about, and process information. You need time to figure something out for yourself. If you are impulsive, once something is clear, you will be impatient to move on to the next step. Whether you are reflective or impulsive makes a difference in how you study.

Some teachers are reflective; their style of teaching will encourage you to think about the subject. Other teachers are more impulsive; they tell you, "Do this, do that, do the other thing." Your style of learning will fit more naturally with a professor of like style.

Turn to the chart at the end of this chapter. In each category: environmental, emotional, sociological, physical, and psychological, determine where you fit. What kind of learner are you? What do you need? How do you best absorb and retain information?

VIII. APPLY YOURSELF

Now that you know yourself, insofar as learning styles are concerned, you're ready for the next step, which is applying yourself.

Make learning meaningful. One way to make learning easier and more efficient is to relate it to something in your life. Or relate the information to your future profession or career. Make it personal.

Hook learning to previous knowledge. Information is more readily retained and recalled if it is hooked to something you already know.

> *Studying needs to be something you do continuously, not just the last night before the test.*

Make learning into a picture. A picture in this sense is not necessarily something you can visualize; rather, it is determining, as you hear and see, how you will organize and label that information. Information is easier to recall when it is put into categories.

Schematic mapping helps you retain information. Outlining is a form of schematic mapping; diagramming is another. In schematic mapping, you take several details and reorganize them; you structure them; you put them together in a picture where you categorize and label them. The information is thus easier to retain and recall when needed.

A mnemonic device is another way to picture information. In music, the famous mnemonic devices for lines and spaces are: **F—A—C—E,** and Every Good Boy Does Fine.

You can make up your own mnemonic device to remember information for a test.

React and interact with learning. Get involved with what you are learning.

The more you can talk about it, write about it, think about it, the more the information is enhanced, making it easier to recall and retain.

Make learning a continuous process. This is a positive way of saying, "Don't wait until the night before the test and try to learn everything in three hours." To learn something and know it well, the process should be continuous. Work on it for a while, then come back and see how much you remember.

IX. BELIEVE IN YOURSELF

This last step is all important. After getting to know yourself and discovering ways to apply yourself, the final step is believing in yourself.

Philippians 4:13 is a comfort and encouragement, as well as a promise.

> *"I can do all things through Christ, who strengthens me."*

Remember that help is available to you in Christ. Make that help an important part of studying. When you have a tough assignment, take time to think, to pray, to read the Scriptures, and to let God strengthen you. Your prayer might be something like this: "Clear my mind, Lord. Help me to organize this and present myself in the best possible way."

> *Prayer and a conscious attitude of depending on Christ is an important part of your learning strategy.*

Dr. William Purkey illustrated this point so well in a speech given at a national convention of educators. He stated that in one of his earlier publications he made the statement, "I CAN is just as important as IQ." However, he wanted it known that this statement was wrong. Actually, "I CAN is one hundred times more important than IQ." An "I Can" attitude is part of believing in yourself.

You CAN do it. Your style of learning may be different from the person sitting next to you in class. Your way of processing information may be a little different from the way the teacher says you should do it. But if you believe in yourself, and you believe that you can do it, you will succeed.

✔ Know yourself.

✔ Apply yourself.

✔ Believe in yourself.

You will be a successful learner.

LEARNING STYLES MODEL
DESIGNED BY DR. RITA DUNN DR. KENNETH DUNN

ELEMENTS

Stimuli				
Environmental	SOUND	LIGHT	TEMPERATURE	DESIGN
Emotional	MOTIVATION	PERSISTENCE	RESPONSIBILITY	STRUCTURE
Sociological	SELF	PAIR / PEERS	TEAM	ADULT / VARIED
Physical	PERCEPTUAL	INTAKE	TIME	MOBILITY
Psychological	GLOBAL / ANALYTIC	HEMISPHERICITY	IMPULSIVE / REFLECTIVE	

Simultaneous or Successive Processing

Chart used by permission of Rita and Kenneth Dunn,
Center for the Study of Learning and Teaching Styles,
St. Johns University, Utopia Parkway, Jamica, New York 11439

49

Chapter Three
Discussion Questions and Exercises

Analyze Your Learning Styles

Auditory and Visual Learners

Check one answer for each question.

1. I prefer to learn by
   - ☐ a. listening to a lecture.
   - ☐ b. reading the textbook.

2. I prefer to learn by
   - ☐ a. listening to an explanation.
   - ☐ b. watching a demonstration.

3. When listening to a lecture,
   - ☐ a. I take few notes.
   - ☐ b. I take many notes.

4. I tend to remember people's
   - ☐ a. names but forget their faces.
   - ☐ b. faces but forget their names.

5. I like a classroom seat where I
   - ☐ a. hear what is said.
   - ☐ b. see what is going on.

6. Graphs, charts and diagrams
   - ☐ a. confuse me.
   - ☐ b. are interesting to me.

7. I like to read maps.
   - ☐ a. yes
   - ☐ b. no

8. I don't mind studying with noise in the background.

   ☐ a. yes
   ☐ b. no

The "a" responses are usually checked by auditory learners, and the "b" responses by visual learners. If you checked about the same number of both "a" and "b," you are probably one of the majority who prefer visual and auditory methods of learning about equally.

Tactile and Kinesthetic Learners

Check the boxes in front of the statements that describe you or that you believe to be true concerning you.

☐ When I was in grade school, I could usually find an excuse to get up and move around the room.

☐ When I study, I need to take frequent breaks.

☐ The best part of science classes is doing the experiments in the lab.

☐ I prefer a job that keeps me on my feet, moving from place to place, rather than one that gives me a chance to sit most of the time.

☐ Engineering and construction work interest me.

☐ I derive great enjoyment in typing or doing computer work.

☐ If I bought a new VCR, I would probably try to figure out how it works by playing with it rather than reading the owner's manual.

If you checked five or more of these statements, you are strongly oriented toward kinesthetic and tactile learning.

Environment Preferences

Check the answer that best describes you.

1. I do my best work
   - ☐ a. in the morning
   - ☐ b. in the afternoon
   - ☐ c. in the evening

2. I prefer to study
   - ☐ a. at a desk, sitting in chair
   - ☐ b. in an armchair, a sofa or a bed

3. I study best in a
   - ☐ a. dormitory or bedroom
   - ☐ b. living room
   - ☐ c. kitchen
   - ☐ d. library
   - ☐ e. cafeteria

4. I like to study in a place with
   - ☐ a. bright light
   - ☐ b. medium light
   - ☐ c. dim light

5. I prefer to study in a room that is
   - ☐ a. hot
   - ☐ b. warm
   - ☐ c. cool
   - ☐ d. cold

6. I learn best when I study with
   - ☐ a. loud background music playing
   - ☐ b. soft background music playing
   - ☐ c. no background music playing

7. When I study, the sound of voices or noise
   ☐ a. doesn't bother me
   ☐ b. bothers me a little
   ☐ c. makes it impossible for me to study

8. When studying, I like to
   ☐ a. drink a beverage
   ☐ b. chew gum
   ☐ c. eat snack food
   ☐ d. eat a meal
   ☐ d. avoid eating and drinking

9. I prefer to study
   ☐ a. by myself
   ☐ b. with one other person
   ☐ c. with a group of people

10. I study most efficiently when
   ☐ a. I am under the pressure of a deadline
   ☐ b. there is no rush to meet a deadline

Experiment with a variety of environmental conditions to find the optimum study conditions for yourself.

Describe Your Learning Style

1. List several learning characteristics that apply to you.

_____

_____

_____

_____

_____

_____

2. Describe what would be your perfect study environment.

_____

_____

_____

_____

_____

3. Describe your present study environment.

_____

_____

_____

_____

_____

_____

4. List ways you can improve your study environment.

_____

_____

_____

_____

_____

_____

5. Which professors do you find it easier to relate to? Do you think this has to do with their teaching style and your learning style?

_____

_____

_____

_____

_____

♥   ♥   ♥

Scripture and Prayer

You created my inmost being; you knit me together in my mother's womb. I praise you because I am fearfully and wonderfully made; your works are wonderful, I know that full well. Psalm 139:13,14

Heavenly Father,

I thank you that you created me in your image—an image so vast, so complex, and so multi-faceted. And how thankful I am that even though I am created in your image, I am also created a unique human being with individual abilities, gifts, and traits.

Lord, help me to take advantage of the research others have made into the different styles of learning so that I can discover my individual strengths in the learning process. Help me to know and appreciate myself as an individual that I might better apply myself to the job of gaining a college education. Please help me to maintain an "I Can" attitude, always believing in myself because I believe in you.

amen

How to Take Tests

Making the Grade

4

How to Take Tests

Practicing good test-taking techniques will greatly enhance your college success.

Few people like to take tests. Yet, during your college career, you will spend approximately 40% of your time preparing for or taking tests. Therefore, the more you can learn about the proper approach to taking tests, the more successful your college career will be.

Tests come in several shapes and sizes:

✔ the intimidating weekly tests

✔ the stressful pop quiz

✔ the excruciating mid-term

✔ the paradoxical take-home test

✔ the ultimate assault: cumulative final exams

A good test should have the following characteristics: It should be a reasonable and timely command to study. It should measure what you have been taught. It should be fair and balanced—neither super-hard nor super-easy. It should be given as a classroom exam and not as a homework assignment.

I. THE PURPOSE OF TESTS

1. Enforce study of course content

Even the most motivated students will not study unless there is a test. Tests are a timely command to study. Tests motivate you to study the course content.

2. Evaluate level and quality of individual learning

It's difficult for the professor to tell, from classroom observation alone, who is learning and who is not. However, individual efforts can be assessed with a test.

An analogy of my twin daughters illustrates the difficulty of ascertaining true progress. When they were babies, I would spread a blanket in the middle of the living room floor to let them crawl. Didi was the more determined twin; she would strain and inch along, trying to reach her toys. Mimi was more laid-back. She would just lie there and smile. Then when she saw me looking at her, she would flap her arms and her legs. If I didn't look carefully, I would think that both were crawling. But if I measured their progress, I could tell that only Didi was moving from one spot to the next. Mimi would stay in the same place, just flapping her arms and legs.

When I am lecturing, sometimes I can't tell which students are really making progress and which are just making the motions. I am not sure which students are prepared and which are not. Giving a test enables me to evaluate what each student has learned.

3. Provide feedback for students

Not only do tests show students areas of improvement, but tests also help students to maintain their achievement.

The Bible speaks of a final examination in heaven where the works of each believer will be tested.

> *"There is going to come a time of testing at Christ's Judgment Day to see what kind of material each builder has used. Everyone's work will be put through the fire so that all can see whether or not it keeps its value, and what was really accomplished."*
> I Corinthians 3:13 (TLB)

A synonym for the word *test* is *examination*. It comes from the Latin word *examinare,* which means to weigh accurately. Therefore, a scholar's battle cry is "Get weighed regularly!"

David's prayer in Psalm 26:2 says, *"Test me, O Lord, and try me. Examine my heart and my mind."* So our scholar's prayer would be, "Test me. Try me. Examine me."

4. Test taking has three parts

Merlin's, *A Guide For Survival* expounds on the three parts of test taking: before, during, and after.

Before: This incorporates prior periods of preparation, including the night before the examination. Adequate preparation can reduce test anxiety and make study more effective.

During: The actual writing of your test. There are techniques that will maximize your responses and enhance their quality in the eyes of the examiner. The result—a better grade.

After: The day you receive your graded paper. You may think that after you take your test, you are done. No. The third part, after, is also important. There are principles that will guide you through recovery, better preparing you for the next test and helping you maintain a high level of achievement.

II. BEFORE THE EXAM

1. Bad cram vs. good cram

The word "cramming" has taken on a bad connotation over the years. Cramming has come to mean staying up all night before the exam, trying to stuff five chapters of material in one night. That is bad cramming. However, there is also good cramming.

A good cram is an effort-filled study session designed to stuff many concepts, facts, and material into your mind just before you need them.

Professionals cram. Most professors cram before giving a lecture. They review the material and make notes, filling their minds with information they feel will be most useful for their students. Lawyers probably cram and fill their minds with pertinent information when they argue a case in court.

Cramming is good when it is an effort-filled study session, designed to stuff a lot of material into your head just before you need it. A good cram is built on prior periods of preparation.

- ✔ Read the assigned work continuously—even before the lecture.

- ✔ Complete homework assignments regularly—as soon as they are given, while the information is still fresh in your mind.

- ✔ Attend classes religiously. It's good to have the same kind of commitment to attending class that we have to attending church. Every Sunday we go to church. Every class session, we go to class.

✔ Be in class daily. Missing one session of class takes at least two sessions to catch up.

✔ Be on time. Being ten minutes late causes you to lose more than the ten minutes, because you try to do several things at once to catch up. You try to copy the notes you missed, try to discover where the professor is in the lesson plan, and try to calculate and understand the key points the professor is making. None of these will be done effectively. Also, when you are late, you interrupt the class and cause distractions for the other students and your professor. So be on time—or even a few minutes early.

✔ Sit in the front, or as near to the front as possible. It is more difficult to see the board and absorb what the professor is saying when you sit in the back of the room.

A good cram is a climax to a long period of reliable work, rather than a last-minute way to save your hide.

---

2. How to cram effectively

Familiarize yourself with the bulk of the material assigned for the test. The best method for this is to follow the professor's test scope.

A test scope is usually given three to five days before the test. This scope will include the chapters covered in the test, the formulas that should be memorized, and the types of questions that may be asked. Most professors will also include sample problems the students should be able to work to do well on the test.

Make a list of the order in which you will study the material. This includes lecture notes, textbook chapters, and outside reading. Your lecture notes are the most important and most reliable source. Lecture notes represent the organized material the professors rate important. Material they consider important will naturally be covered on the test. Lecture notes should be given priority study time.

Look through the textbook chapters. Then, if you still have time, outside materials can broaden your knowledge. Study guides are also helpful, because they have extra problems for practice.

Old tests can sometimes be useful. If you know someone who took the professor's class before, it is all right to look at some of the old tests. However, be warned: old tests can give a false sense of security.

Students have a tendency to study only the material on the old test, and professors like to change tests. Old tests should never be the only material studied.

Never omit studying a potential topic; always aim for 100%. Do not try to guess what will be on the test and what will not. Study all the material.

3. The S3RQ study method

S — Survey
3R — Read, Recite, Review
Q — Question

Survey, or scan, the entire chapter, picking out key words. Read the main headings, and then read the chapter summaries.

Read the material by understanding; underline or highlight important phrases.

Recite the material. Close the textbook and recite to see how much you retain.

Review; open the book again and check how much you recited correctly.

Question. Ask, "What will the professor probably ask from this chapter?" Then list all the questions. Pretend that you are the teacher and write down the questions you would ask the students. Your questions will usually be similar to the test questions.

4. Active studying

Passive studying could be described as reading with one eye and watching television with the other. Nothing is gained, even with several hours of passive reading.

Active studying incorporates several things:

✔ Study the chapter prior to attending the lectures.

✔ Participate in the class discussions.

✔ Do the problems as soon as they are assigned.

✔ Apply what you are learning to your daily life and surroundings.

In my Chemistry Class, I explained that the use of polymers permeates our daily lives. A typical student might have a sandwich wrapped in a polyethylene plastic, stored in an insulated lunch pail made of polystyrene, and will probably drink water from a polyvinylchloride pipe. The student also could have worn a polyacrylnitril outfit, and sat in a chair made of polyacrylate material, glued together with a polytetrachloroethylene.

5. Get help

Ask questions and get help from your instructor or tutor. Professors and instructors usually have their office hours posted on their doors. They make themselves available to help you. Seek their help when you need it.

In most colleges and universities the Department of Education will have a tutoring service where students can sign up for a tutor. They also will have a math center where math majors can help students with math problems.

6. Study groups

A research team at UCLA wanted to discover why a certain group of people—Asian-Americans in this case—did extremely well in math. In their observations of this group, the research team found that the Asian-Americans studied in groups. The students in the groups also took turns playing "teacher," where they would explain something to others in the group.

Explaining something to another person is an excellent way to determine if you know the material. So play "teacher" and study with a group of students.

A common quotation says, "Genius is 1% inspiration, but 99% perspiration." Here's another, "Preparation is 95% of test success. The other 5% is going to class and writing it down."

---

7. Memorization

Students often complain that teachers expect too much when they ask them to memorize selected material. These students do not realize the wonderful memory capacity they possess. The memory capacity of a ten year old child is greater than the memory capacity of the thousands of computers it would take to fill the Empire State Building.

God has given you a wonderful "computer." Store it with information. Memorize selected material.

Memorization plays a significant role in learning. In the sciences, students must memorize many formulas. Do you realize that each formula you are required to memorize represents the hard work of scientists? Your work and life are easier because scientists worked out these formulas and theories. So learn the formulas and use them.

We have all used memorization since we were small children. Most of us probably used "Roy G. Biv" as a device to memorize the colors in the rainbow: Red, Orange, Yellow, Green, Blue, Indigo, Violet. That's just one type of mnemonic device to help memorize selected material.

8. Maintain an alert mind and a cheerful attitude

Athletes know that part of the preparation for a game is to sleep well the night before and to eat well.

Scholars, like athletes, are also in training. Intellectual effort is best served by a well-nourished and well-rested body. Students who stay out all night before an exam come to class not only physically tired, but also emotionally and mentally tired. They can't think clearly.

Students who do not eat a well balanced breakfast the day of the exam will be hungry, and this will be a distraction.

Prepare for tests like an athlete prepares for a game. Have a well-nourished body and a well-rested body.

While the following Bible verse is usually applied to athletes, we also can apply it to scholars.

"I have fought the good fight. I have finished the race. I have kept the faith. Now there is in store for me the crown of righteousness...."
2 Timothy 4:7-8 (NIV)

We have studied. We have fought the good fight. We are now coming into the exam room. We want to get our crown of righteousness—the *A+*.

III. DURING THE EXAM

Certain techniques can help you during the test; they give you the extra edge that turns a *B-* to a *B+*, or even a *B+* to an *A*.

✔ If the test is lengthy—if it's more than 90 minutes—bring a candy bar to supplement your physical energy. After the first hour, you begin to get tired.

✔ If you are tense, it's better to chew gum than to tap your pencil. Tapping a pencil distracts others in the classroom.

✔ Avoid making excuses. Sometimes students come in on the day of the exam with lame excuses, such as "I have something in my eye. Do I have to take the test?"

Your professors have already heard most of the excuses; seldom will they excuse you from the test.

✔ Always start with the question you know best, even if it is not the first one. Confidence will build as you write something you know well.

1. Multiple choice tests

Eliminate, do not guess wildly. If there are four choices, you can probably spot one or two that do not belong—eliminate them first. Your choice narrows, and your chances improve.

Do not second-guess yourself. Once you start answering and moving down the line of questions, do not go back and correct the answers. According to the psychology of signal detection theory, first impulses are usually correct.

Do not agonize over one impossible item. If a test includes one hundred multiple choice questions, each is worth only one point. If you get stuck, put a question mark beside it and go on to the next. Don't spend ten minutes on one difficult item.

Avoid humorous or illogical choices. Professors sometimes put in one or two humorous answers. Avoid them. Most of the time the student says, "Oh, this is so cute. Isn't this cute?" Usually it's a wrong answer, so avoid humorous or illogical choices.

Be a question detective. Use information from other parts of the test. Look for the answer in another part of the test.

"All of these" and "none of these." Avoid these choices unless you are absolutely sure. They are usually distractions.

True and false. Choose "true" when in doubt, or if you have no clue. It is more difficult to form a false statement than a true one. This is strictly a last-ditch effort when you do not know.

2. Essay tests

Do you know why students do not like essay tests? With multiple choice or true and false, it is possible sometimes to guess the correct answer. With essay tests you have to know the material.

Good essay answers should follow the age-old formula for good communication. They should include three parts:

- ✔ Preview: tell them what you are going to tell them.
- ✔ Content: tell them.
- ✔ Summary: tell them what you have just told them.

Preview: A statement, usually in one sentence or two, telling what territory you will cover in your answer. Previews should be short, to the point, attractive, and interesting.

Content: An elaboration or development of the plan stated in the opening. Use several paragraphs; each must have an opening sentence and just one main idea. Other ideas belong in other paragraphs. Do not write everything in one long, rambling paragraph—it's hard to read and hard to correct.

Underline important ideas. Professors correct many essays, and anything you do such as underlining key points or using an outline form should earn you a better grade. This shows the professor that you have organization skills.

Sprinkle with concrete examples. For example, an essay-type answer in chemistry should include something concrete: a chemical reaction, an equation, a chart, or a graph showing transition.

Write clearly, legibly and calmly. No matter how good the idea, if the professor can't read the handwriting, the grade will be lower.

Mix sentence structure. Compound, complex sentences are fine, but do not use the same style throughout the essay. Use short sentences occasionally to change pace and make the essay more interesting.

Pace yourself. This is very important. Students sometimes forget to watch the time while taking an exam. If there are ten essay questions to answer in a fifty minute class, do not spend forty minutes on the first two. Regardless of how beautiful your answers are on the first two, you will fail the test because you ran out of time. So pace yourself.

Summary. Reiterate and summarize the main point that you have written in the body of the essay. A good essay should have preview, content, and summary.

3. Taking a math or chemistry test

- ✔ Write down the information you are given.

- ✔ Write down what you want to find or prove. Write down any formulas, definitions or theorems you will need.

- ✔ Try to use all the relevant information that you are given.

You can get a clue to the problem by estimating what the answer would be. Write down your estimated answer. Next try to work backwards from the conclusion to get a hint of what process you should use. Then compare your final answer with your first estimate to see if your answer makes sense. If it's completely illogical, you probably won't get any points. This process works for math and chemistry.

Helpful books are, *Mastering Mathematics and How to Be a Great Math Student* by Richard Manning Smith; *How to Study Chemistry* by Erwin Becker.

4. Controlling test anxiety

Do you suffer from mental block when you see the test paper? The cause of mental block is test anxiety and inadequate preparation. However, there are some things you can do to control test anxiety:

Focus on the problem at hand—the test. Be task-focused, rather than self-focused. Do not focus on yourself. Don't say, "Oh, no. I'm going to fail this test. I know I'm not going to get this degree. I know that my father's going to kill me." Instead focus on the task. "This is a task I must do right now. I'll approach it calmly and logically." One way to focus on the task is to jot down key points you have memorized; do this on scratch paper or the back of your test paper. Then then go back and organize the points you wrote down.

Stop comparing yourself with other students around you. It can be discouraging when, five minutes after the test, someone stands up, turns in his paper, and walks off with a big smile on his face. Do not compare yourself with that person. He probably gave up because he didn't know the answers, and his big smile was just a front. Never compare yourself with others in the class.

Never permit the first question in the test to throw you. Simply go to the next one if you can't answer the first. Find a question you know and start answering it. It isn't required that you answer the first question first; you can always come back. When you start with a question you know, confidence will build.

Avoid panicky self-talk. Don't say, "When I go out of here, I'm doomed. I'll never get back because I'm going to get an *F*." Stop saying things like that. Think positive.

Learn behavioral relaxation and deep breathing exercises. Most professors would not mind if you stood up and stretched a little. Relax, and you will think better.

Share your distress with someone you trust. If you constantly have overwhelming test anxiety, let someone you trust know about it. Let your professors or your mentor students know you are having a problem with mental block. Ask them to help you prepare better.

Don't hesitate to ask your professor to clarify a question. Most professors will try to clarify the question if they can do so without telling the answer.

Come to the test 200% prepared. Then if you are having mental block or you are nervous and lose 100%, you still get 100%.

Start each test with a silent prayer. After you get the test paper, take a few minutes, shut your eyes and say, "Lord,

I studied for this test. I did everything my professor said. I did my best. I ate a nourishing breakfast. I rested last night. So, Lord, help me to do my best today. Give me a calm heart and a clear mind so that I can do my very best. Amen."

IV. AFTER THE EXAM

What do you do when you have finished taking the test? Do you run up, throw the test paper on the professor's desk, and say, "I am out of here!" No. If it's possible, ask the professor if you can take the question paper with you. Then you can research the test questions again—this time without fear.

If the professor will not let you take the question paper, then as soon as you go out of the room jot down as many questions as you can remember.

Next, whether you have the question paper or the questions that you jotted down, review the material in the privacy of your own home. Preview your test grade. Look over your paper and say, "I got this one correctly. I didn't get this one." Sum up the grade. You'll get an idea how well you did. And if need be, if you missed several, and if you want to scream, go ahead. You are alone, and you won't disturb anybody. Then, it's over! Because you have previewed your test grade, you are no longer traumatized.

Also, looking at the question paper helps you develop an ear for the style of the teacher's questioning. Look at the tests you have already taken. What kind of questions did the professor ask? Is the test highly structured? Is it based mostly on his lectures? Is it completely off the wall? Or does it look like he wants you to be creative or to apply what you have learned? Develop an ear for the teacher's style of questioning.

Remember, recovering from exams is preparation for the next one. Recovering properly gives you a head start for the next test. One aid to test recovery is to reward yourself when the test is finished. Do something nice for yourself. You deserve it.

When you receive your graded test paper, do more than just look at the grade, wad it up, and throw it away. Take time to read the teacher's comments, and learn from your mistakes. Remember— there is always the next test.

Use the graded test to help you identify ways to improve your study habits for the next test.

> *"The simple inherit folly, but the prudent,* [the hard working] *are crowned with knowledge."*
> Proverbs 14:18 (NIV)

That's what education is all about—to get knowledge.

Chapter Four

Discussion Questions and Exercises

1. Review Checklist.

   ■ What material will be covered in the test?

   ■ What specific suggestions does the instructor have about what you should be studying in preparation for the test?

   ■ Will you be allowed to refer to any books, handouts, or notes during the test?

   ■ Will you be allowed to use a calculator or other equipment during the test?

   ■ Will equal importance be given to information in the textbook, classnotes, and handouts, or will greater importance be given to one of these?

   ■ What is the format of the test? True or False? Matching Type? Essay? Problem Solving?

   ■ When and where will the test be given?

   ■ How many minutes/hours will the test be?

   ■ Will the test be similar to earlier tests given by the instructor?

2. During the test, mentally go through this check list.

   ■ REDUCE ANXIETY with a short word of prayer, reminding yourself that you have prepared thoroughly before the test, and that God will help you to do your best.

   ■ SURVEY the test to see what types of questions you must answer, whether any page is missing, and whether questions are printed on both sides of the paper.

   ■ READ the directions carefully and follow them exactly.

   ■ LISTEN attentively to everything the instructor says before and during the test.

   ■ PLAN your test-taking time so you will have time to answer all the question you know, maximizing the potential for best grade by making sure the questions that are worth more are answered.

- **START** by answering the question you know best to build up your confidence.

- **ANSWER** all the questions to the best of your ability.

- **CHECK** your answers, but be careful not to change correct answers to incorrect ones.

3. List three actions you will take to overcome any anxiety you feel about taking tests. Then schedule a specific time for taking each action.

a. _____

_____

_____

_____

_____

b. _____

_____

_____

_____

_____

c. _____

_____

_____

_____

_____

4. Score yourself on test-taking strategies by using these guidelines:
   Always — 5 points
   Often — 4 points
   Somewhat true — 3 points
   Seldom true — 2 points
   Never true — 1 point

In each of the following statements, indicate the number that best describes you. Then add your total score.

____ I feel confident and calm during an exam.

____ I plan my time during exams and I am able to complete the test.

____ I am able to predict test questions,

____ I adapt my test-taking strategy to the kind of test I am taking.

____ I understand the test questions and can answer them completely and accurately.

____ I start reviewing for tests at least two weeks in advance and review regularly.

_____ Total Score

Discussion Questions

1. What are your problem areas? How can you find help?

   _____

   _____

   _____

2. What specific study skills are you lacking? How can you strengthen those skills?

   _____

   _____

3. What should you do to minimize test anxiety?

_____

_____

_____

4. What specific steps will you take to improve your grades?

_____

_____

_____

♥ ♥ ♥

Scripture and Prayer

Do not be anxious about anything, but in everything, by prayer and petition, with thanksgiving, present your requests to God. And the peace of God, which transcends all understanding, will guard your hearts and your minds in Christ Jesus. Philippians 4:6,7

Heavenly Father,

Thank you for the information in this chapter. Thank you that it will enable me to better prepare for tests, to remain calm during tests, and to focus on each step of the test in the most efficient manner.

Help me to form and maintain good study habits and to plan ahead and make time for test preparation. Remind me, Lord, that you are always with me, and you have promised to send your Holy Spirit—the Helper—to all believers. And, Lord, if I sense fear and anxiety rising when I'm in the midst of a test, remind me of the words of the psalmist, "When I am afraid I will trust in you." Remind me, Lord, to give thanks in all things—even tests—for thankfulness is a key that unlocks my greatest potential.

amen

Making Friends

Don Thoren

5

Making Friends

Explore a wide range of new friendship possibilities by carefully observing others for clues to how they like to be treated.

When entering a new environment, like college, you leave many friends behind. Even knowing you will make new ones, most of us are still nervous about where to begin, what kind of people to seek out, and how to do it. Let's begin with quick, short answers to these questions and later discuss "how to do it" in greater detail.

✔ First: making new friends begins immediately and happens most frequently during the first few weeks when the largest number of people are consciously looking for new friends.

✔ Next: the kind of people you meet first will be people who have many things in common with you such as: age, dormitory assignment, classes attending, academic level within courses, teachers, clubs joined, part-time job holders, attend the same church, academic advisors, etc.

✔ Last: the question of how to establish rapport, and if desired, explore building a friendship out of an acquaintance, is founded on a simple guideline: "Closely observing the predominant behaviors of the other person will give you many clues about the kinds of behaviors he/she prefers and will best respond to. "

This grouping of preferences is called a COMFORT ZONE. When your behaviors are similar to it, the other person is more comfortable and eager to explore a potential friendship with you.

I. THE COMFORT ZONE

Let me illustrate the COMFORT ZONE idea with a story I use in all my seminars on "Interpersonal Effectiveness" with my corporate clients. (You see, your parents or your friends who get moved around by their employers continue to experience the same challenge of making new friends.)

For this story, picture a family at a picnic by the seashore. People are walking around, talking, eating, playing and enjoying the day. A five year old boy is eating his lunch, God's finest culinary creation—a peanut butter and jelly sandwich. The boy notices some movement down by the edge of the water. And, lo and behold, out on the beach comes the first big sea turtle the boy has ever seen.

With children there are usually one of two reactions when they see a strange animal—either they are terrified and want to get away from it, or they are magnetized and want to make it a friend. This five year old boy knew how to make a friend of an animal. You do

what? You feed it! And with God's finest culinary creation, the child runs to share the peanut butter sandwich and make a new friend.

Now, let's switch our thought to the turtle. It is just beginning to get its land legs, blinking its eyes while getting used to the light. All of a sudden it hears this thump, thump, thump and feels the vibrations from the boy's feet running toward it.

The boy, arriving at the turtle with a shriek of delight, shoves the sandwich right in front of where the turtle's head ... used to be! The turtle has pulled back into its shell. The young boy first thinks, *I'll let him know I'm out here,* so he begins to knock on the shell, but gets no response. The boy then picks up a little piece of driftwood and raps on the turtle's shell! By now, our turtle is cringing on the inside of the shell, about to have cardiac arrest. The last thing the turtle is about to do is stick its head out of that shell to investigate a new friendship!

There is a big moral to this little story: "No matter how good your intentions may be, if your approach is wrong, you can't even give away food."

Where do you suppose the child got the idea that this turtle would respond to a bite of the sandwich and then play on the beach? Perhaps from experiences with the family dog?

While you and I know that turtles are very different from puppy dogs, this little boy did not know that. However, once this difference is explained, the boy will know that to approach and make friends with a turtle is very different from making friends with a puppy dog.

II. OBSERVE PREDOMINANT BEHAVIOR

But the bigger lesson, whether meeting animals or people, is to observe their predominant behavior for clues about how to approach them within their COMFORT ZONE as the first step to gaining the opportunity to explore a potential friendship. In the "turtle" story, it would have been sad if the child had not learned this guideline and had never again attempted friendship with a turtle simply because the first approach was wrong.

While you too, in spite of good intentions, may use the wrong approach initially, you can learn from it and have more confidence about again approaching the same person—only differently.

The Apostle Paul, who probably made more new friends than anyone of his era, is my source for suggesting this guideline to you. In I Corinthians 9:19-21, Paul says:

"Though I am free from all men, I have made myself a slave to all, that I might win the more. To the Jews, I become as a Jew, in order to win the Jews; to those under the law I become as one under the law—though not being myself under the law—that I might win those under the law...to the weak I become weak that I might win the weak...I do it all for the sake of the gospel...."

It is important to note that Paul did not lie or manipulate the truth of the gospel message. Rather, as a messenger, he greatly expanded his COMFORT ZONE of behaviors to be able to build rapport with vastly different people to facilitate their receipt of God's Word. His observations of their behavior as Jews, legalistic, weak, etc., gave him (and can for you) the clues of how to approach them. Perhaps Paul had learned the moral, "No matter how good your intentions may be, if your approach is wrong you can't even give away food!"

Expand your comfort zone and build rapport with many people.

III. EXPANDING AND EXPLORING RELATIONSHIPS

Any fear or apprehension you have about meeting new people is absolutely natural. Usually all of us need some friends who share our COMFORT ZONE, but people whose COMFORT ZONE may be very different can become friends who stimulate creative new ideas and important new insights. Therefore, you can expand your range of possibilities by learning how to better observe behavior. These skills will add to your confidence in approaching people to explore relationships.

In the simple terms of the turtle story, did the turtle offer any clues? How fast did it move? Did it bark? Does it make sense that the child would have experienced more success with slow movements and fewer squeals of delight? (And maybe even a piece of raw fish rather than the magnificent peanut butter and jelly sandwich!)

With this understanding of the basic guideline of how to make friends, let's make a transition from turtles to people and describe predominant behavior patterns you can look for to identify a potential new friend's COMFORT ZONE. As you look to differences in people, you are not looking for goods or bads—just differences.

I have taught this model of different COMFORT ZONES to employees and managers of organizations throughout the United States and Canada with the goal of helping them to recognize *and* appreciate people in each of the COMFORT ZONES—including their own.

Illustration A (at end of chapter) defines the "Emotional Content" behavioral dimension and lists contrasting clues for both Reserved and Emotional behavior. Note: all people are sometimes emotional, sometimes reserved, and sometimes in the middle. What you are looking for is predominance—how people behave most of the time.

✔ Circle the clues you think your current friends would use to describe you most of the time. (Remember, there is nothing good or bad about reserved or emotional.) The clues provide contrast, such as serious vs. playful or embarrassed, limited use of hands vs. uses hands freely, etc. Circle only one of the contrasting pairs.

✔ Now use checks to describe one of your friends. Did you get more checks under **Reserved** or under **Emotional?**

Illustration B (at end of chapter) defines the "Discussion Approach" behavioral dimension and provides contrasting clues for both **Questioner** and **Teller** behavior. Again, people are a mixture, there is neither good or bad, and you are looking for predominance. Use circles to describe yourself, then checks for a friend, as a way of getting familiar with the descriptions. By the way, there is a good chance that many of your circles will be the same as your friend's checks—get the point?

Illustration C (at end of chapter) is the COMFORT ZONE grid formed by displaying Emotional Content at right angles to Discussion Approach to create an interrelationship. The four COMFORT ZONES become :

✔ Reserved Questioner

✔ Reserved Teller

✔ Emotional Teller

✔ Emotional Questioner

For examples of the COMFORT ZONE differences that may be helpful to you, consider these from popular TV shows:

In Happy Days, remember how Fonzie the Reserved (in control) Teller (as in

tells others) was the macho man who had all the answers. Richie the Emotional (always elated or worried) Questioner (What do you think, Fonzie?) always wanted to be liked and not hurt anyone's feelings.

In the Cosby Show, Denise the Emotional Teller talked considerably of her emotional reactions to life while Theo (when he was younger) the Reserved Questioner was the more quiet, analytical child who was continually trying to figure things out.

Does it occur to you that these shows were popular for so long because everyone had a character he or she could relate to? Also to keep our interest, each character would frequently step out of his/her COMFORT ZONE to cope with

Happy Days

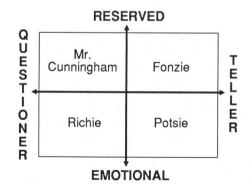

The Cosby Show

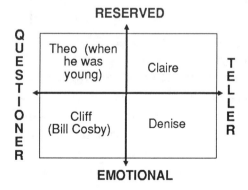

some special situation. In the Cosby Show, Claire controlled most decisions but frequently either Cliff would become more of a Teller to solve a problem or Claire would become less of a Teller and follow the advice of someone else.

If you follow the guideline of carefully observing others for the clues of how they like to be treated, you can effectively explore a wide range of new friendship possibilities.

Naturally, after a friendship develops there is less concern over interpersonal behavior compatibility, and differences can be stimulating rather than uncomfortable.

When I am speaking in front of an audience, I will often ask a very reserved looking person to come to the front of the room and tell me something about himself. As he talks I begin to shuffle my feet so I am getting closer to him. I touch his arm and later put my hand on his shoulder. He begins shuffling backward and either blushes or turns pale, and sometimes is even unable to continue the discussion with me. As the audience and the other person observe what I am doing, we all have a good laugh.

In real life, I would have completely destroyed any opportunity to make a friend of that person because my behavior made him so uncomfortable. However, if I had observed the clues from his behavior I would have kept my distance. I would not have put my hand on his shoulder (even if these are normal behaviors in my COMFORT ZONE. Then I would have earned the opportunity to explore a relationship.

While you may find it somewhat difficult and uncomfortable to initially step out of your COMFORT ZONE to keep the other person comfortable, the reward is that your message gets heard (I Corinthians 9:19-23).

IV. PREPARING FOR SUCCESSFUL EMPLOYMENT

Another reason to begin developing these interpersonal skills while making friends in college is that it will prepare you for successful employment. Employers want good students who can be individually productive, but that is not enough anymore. They will also want you to contribute to high Joint Productivity while working with others in team\group problem analysis and decision making. As an example, each year I conduct a two-day workshop on this topic for the new college hires of Honeywell Corporation. Many of these new employees have technical degrees where they have had to compete for grades. That is okay, but their career will be severely limited if they do not also quickly learn how to cooperatively exchange information and resources which lead to the discovery of creative new ideas.

Perhaps the different COMFORT ZONES are an extension of God's plan to give each of us different gifts. Differences can divide us until we understand them, but then they can greatly enrich our lives and our teamwork results.

Jesus commanded, *"You shall love your neighbor as yourself."* We have learned that isn't easy! It is my prayer that God will use the ideas of this chapter to help you better understand the differences in people's behavior and personalities. Then armed with greater understanding, you will be able to make more friends and love them more!

Illustration A

Comfort Zone - Emotional Content

The amount of feelings and personal reactions included with the message.

RESERVED

Serious
Limited use of the hands
Limited facial expression
More factual "data"
Less personal opinion/reaction

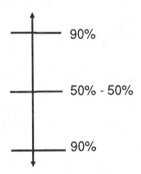

90%

50% - 50%

90%

EMOTIONAL

Playful or embarrassed
Uses hands freely
Considerable facial expression
Less factual "data"
More personal opinion/reaction

Illustration B

Comfort Zone - Discussion Approach

The most predictable technique for exchanging information or influencing other people.

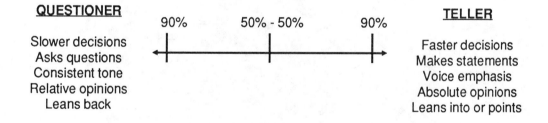

Illustration C

Comfort Zones – The Combinations Formed by Combining Emotional Content and Discussion Approach

RESERVED

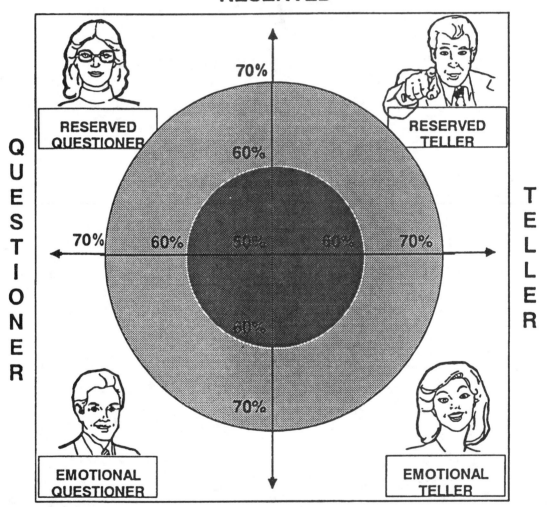

EMOTIONAL

Chapter Five

Discussion Questions and Exercises

1. Where did you rate yourself on Illustration A? _____

   Are you reserved or emotional? _____

   _____

2. How about your friends? Are most of them in your COMFORT ZONE?

   _____

   _____

   _____

3. Think of one person who is quite opposite from you that you would like to get to know better. What steps could you take to explore a friendship with this person?

   _____

   _____

   _____

   _____

4. Can you recall an incident where someone approached you in a way that made you draw back? _____

   _____

   _____

   _____

5. Have you ever made a bad approach to someone? _____

   Did you get a chance to correct it? _____

   _____

♥ ♥ ♥

Scripture and Prayer

*A friend loves at all times...*Proverbs 17:17
...but there is a friend who sticks closer than a brother.
Proverbs 18:24
*He who walks with the wise grows wise....*Proverbs 13:20

Heavenly Father,

It seems so strange to be in this new place, surrounded by people I don't know. I miss the good friends I had in high school. Help me to make new friends on campus. I know that among the people I pass on the way to classes, the people standing in line at the cafeterias, and the people in my classrooms, there must be many who are as eager as I am to make new friends. Help me to be friendly, to reach out to others, to smile at them and speak to them.

Now, I thank you in advance for the special people I will meet and who will become my friends this year and the years ahead. And I thank you that in addition to all my other friends, you are the friend who sticks closer than a brother.

amen

Personality Profile

Created by Fred Littauer

This study of the temperaments has been extremely well received in churches and other groups. It is designed to help you discover more about yourself and why you function the way you do. This analysis is for your personal benefit, but knowing about the temperaments helps you to better understand and deal with family and friends. It helps you to realize that people who are not like you are not wrong, they are just different. Also, opposites attract and we compliment each other. You will probably not be totally in one category, but generally one area will be dominant. Accept yourself as you are and don't waste time wishing you were like someone else. Study your strengths and work to enhance them. Acknowledge your weaknesses and start to overcome them. Remember that *"with God all things are possible"* Mark 10:27.

Personality Profile

Created by Fred Littauer   Name:_____

DIRECTIONS: In <u>each</u> of the following rows of <u>four</u> words across, place an X in front of the one word that <u>most</u> often applies to you. Continue through all forty lines. Be sure each number is marked. If you are not sure of which word "most applies," ask a spouse or a friend, and think of what your answer would have been <u>when you were a child</u>.

Strengths

1	___Adventurous	___Adaptable	___Animated	___Analytical
2	___Persistent	___Playful	___Persuasive	___Peaceful
3	___Submissive	___Self-sacrificing	___Sociable	___Strong-willed
4	___Considerate	___Controlled	___Competitive	___Convincing
5	___Refreshing	___Respectful	___Reserved	___Resourceful
6	___Satisfied	___Sensitive	___Self-reliant	___Spirited
7	___Planner	___Patient	___Positive	___Promoter
8	___Sure	___Spontaneous	___Scheduled	___Shy
9	___Orderly	___Obliging	___Outspoken	___Optimistic
10	___Friendly	___Faithful	___Funny	___Forceful
11	___Daring	___Delightful	___Diplomatic	___Detailed
12	___Cheerful	___Consistent	___Cultured	___Confident
13	___Idealistic	___Independent	___Inoffensive	___Inspiring
14	___Demonstrative	___Decisive	___Dry humor	___Deep
15	___Mediator	___Musical	___Mover	___Mixes easily
16	___Thoughtful	___Tenacious	___Talker	___Tolerant
17	___Listener	___Loyal	___Leader	___Lively
18	___Contented	___Chief	___Chartmaker	___Cute
19	___Perfectionist	___Pleasant	___Productive	___Popular
20	___Bouncy	___Bold	___Behaved	___Balanced

Weaknesses

21	____Blank	____Bashful	____Brassy	____Bossy
22	____Undisciplined	____Unsympathetic	____Unenthusiastic	____Unforgiving
23	____Reticent	____Resentful	____Resistant	____Repetitious
24	____Fussy	____Fearful	____Forgetful	____Frank
25	____Impatient	____Insecure	____Indecisive	____Interrupts
26	____Unpopular	____Uninvolved	____Unpredictable	____Unaffectionate
27	____Headstrong	____Haphazard	____Hard to please	____Hesitant
28	____Plain	____Pessimistic	____Proud	____Permissive
29	____Angered easily	____Aimless	____Argumentative	____Alienated
30	____Naive	____Negative attitude	____Nervy	____Nonchalant
31	____Worrier	____Withdrawn	____Workaholic	____Wants credit
32	____Too sensitive	____Tactless	____Timid	____Talkative
33	____Doubtful	____Disorganized	____Domineering	____Depressed
34	____Inconsistent	____Introvert	____Intolerant	____Indifferent
35	____Messy	____Moody	____Mumbles	____Manipulative
36	____Slow	____Stubborn	____Show-off	____Skeptical
37	____Loner	____Lord over	____Lazy	____Loud
38	____Sluggish	____Suspicious	____Short-tempered	____Scatterbrained
39	____Revengeful	____Restless	____Reluctant	____Rash
40	____Compromising	____Critical	____Crafty	____Changeable

Now transfer all your x's to the corresponding words on the Personality Scoring Sheet (next 2 pages) and add up your totals.

PERSONALITY SCORING SHEET

Name_____

Strengths

	Sanguine Popular	Choleric Powerful	Melancholy Perfect	Phlegmatic Peaceful
1	____Animated	____Adventuorous	____Analytical	____Adaptable
2	____Playful	____Persuasive	____Persistent	____Peaceful
3	____Sociable	____Strong-willed	____Self-sacrificing	____Submissive
4	____Convincing	____Competitive	____Considerate	____Controlled
5	____Refreshing	____Resourceful	____Respectful	____Reserved
6	____Spirited	____Self-reliant	____Sensitive	____Satisfied
7	____Promoter	____Positive	____Planner	____Patient
8	____Spontaneous	____Sure	____Scheduled	____Shy
9	____Optimistic	____Outspoken	____Orderly	____Obliging
10	____Funny	____Forceful	____Faithful	____Friendly
11	____Delightful	____Daring	____Detailed	____Diplomatic
12	____Cheerful	____Confident	____Cultured	____Consistent
13	____Inspiring	____Independent	____Idealistic	____Inoffensive
14	____Demonstrative	____Decisive	____Deep	____Dry humor
15	____Mixes easily	____Mover	____Musical	____Mediator
16	____Talker	____Tenacious	____Thoughtful	____Tolerant
17	____Lively	____Leader	____Loyal	____Listener
18	____Cute	____Chief	____Chartmaker	____Contented
19	____Popoular	____Productive	____Perfectionist	____Pleasant
20	____Bouncy	____Bold	____Behaved	____Balanced
Sub Totals	____	____	____	____

Weaknesses

	Sanguine Popular	Choleric Powerful	Melancholy Perfect	Phlegmatic Peaceful
21	Brassy	Bossy	Bashful	Blank
22	Undisciplined	Unsympathetic	Unforgiving	Unenthusiastic
23	Repetitious	Resistant	Resentful	Reticent
24	Forgetful	Frank	Fussy	Fearful
25	Interrupts	Impatient	Insecure	Indecisive
26	Unpredictable	Unaffectionate	Unpopular	Uninvolved
27	Haphazard	Headstrong	Hard-to-please	Hesitant
28	Permissive	Proud	Pessimistic	Plain
29	Angered easily	Argumentative	Alienated	Aimless
30	Naive	Nervy	Negative attitude	Nonchalant
31	Wants credit	Workaholic	Withdrawn	Worrier
32	Talkative	Tactless	Too sensitive	Timid
33	Disorganized	Domineering	Depressed	Doubtful
34	Inconsistent	Intolerant	Introvert	Indifferent
35	Messy	Manipulative	Moody	Mumbles
36	Show-off	Stubborn	Skeptical	Slow
37	Loud	Lord-over-others	Loner	Lazy
38	Scatterbrained	Short tempered	Suspicious	Sluggish
39	Restless	Rash	Revengeful	Reluctant
40	Changeable	Crafty	Critical	Comprising
Sub totals	——	——	——	——
Grand totals	——	——	——	——

Now, look at the charts on the next two pages. They give you added information on basic temperament traits in relationship to emotions, work, and friends.

Strengths

	Sanguine-Popular	Choleric-Powerful	Melancholy-Perfect	Phlegmatic-Peaceful
E M O T I O N S	Appealing personality Talkative, storyteller Life of the party Good sense of humor Memory for color Physically holds on to listener Emotional and demonstrative Enthusiastic and expressive Cheerful and bubbling over Curious Good on stage Wide-eyed and innocent Lives in the present Changeable disposition Sincere at heart Always a child	Born leader Dynamic and active Compulsive need for change Must correct wrongs Strong-willed and decisive Unemotional Not easily discouraged Independent and self-sufficient Exudes confidence Can run anything	Deep and thoughtful Analytical Serious and purposeful Genius prone Talented and creative Artistic or musical Philosophical and poetic Appreciative of beauty Sensitive to others Self-sacrificing Conscientious Idealistic	Low-key personality Easygoing and relaxed Calm, cool, and collected Patient, well balanced Consistent life Quiet, but witty Sympathetic and kind Keeps emotions hidden Happily reconciled to life All-purpose person
W O R K	Volunteers for jobs Thinks up new activities Looks great on the surface Creative and colorful Has energy and enthusiasm Starts in a flashy way Inspires other to join Charms others to work	Goal oriented Sees the whole picture Organizes well Seeks practical solutions Moves quickly to action Delegates work Insists on production Makes the goal Stimulates activity Thrives on opposition	Schedule oriented Perfectionist, high standards Detail conscious Persistent and thorough Orderly and organized Neat and tidy Economical Sees the problems Finds creative solutions Needs to finish what he starts Likes charts, graphs, figures, lists	Competent and steady Peaceful and agreeable Has administrative ability Mediates problems Avoids conflicts Good under pressure Finds the easy way
F R I E N D S	Makes friends easily Loves people Thrives on compliments Seems exciting Envied by others Doesn't hold grudges Apologizes quickly Prevents dull moments Likes spontaneous activities	Has little need for friends Will work for group activity Will lead and organize Is usually right Excels in emergencies	Makes friends cautiously Content to stay in background Avoids causing attention Faithful and devoted Will listen to complaints Can solve other's problems Deep concern for other people Moved to tears with compassion Seeks ideal mate	Easy to get along with Pleasant and enjoyable Inoffensive Good listener Dry sense of humor Enjoys watching people Has many friends Has compassion and concern

Weaknesses

	Sanguine-Popular	Choleric-Powerful	Melancholy-Perfect	Phlegmatic-Peaceful
E M O T I O N S	Compulsive talker Exaggerates and elaborates Dwells on trivia Can't remember names Scares others off Too happy for some Has restless energy Egotistical Blusters and complains Naive, gets taken in Has loud voice and laugh Controlled by circumstances Gets angry easily Seems phony to some Never grows up	Bossy Impatient Quick-tempered Can't relax Too impetuous Enjoys controversy and arguments Won't give up when losing Comes on too strong Inflexible Is not complimentary Dislikes tears and emotions Is unsympathetic	Remembers the negatives Moody and depressed Enjoys being hurt Has false humility Off in another world Low self-image Has selective hearing Self-centered Too introspective Guilt feelings Persecution complex Tends to hypochondria	Unenthusiastic Fearful and worried Indecisive Avoids responsibility Quiet will of iron Selfish Too shy and reticent Too compromising Self-righteous
W O R K	Would rather talk Forgets obligations Doesn't follow through Confidence fades fast Undisciplined Priorities out of order Decides by feelings Easily distracted Wastes time talking	Little tolerance for mistakes Doesn't analyze details Bored by trivia May make rash decisions May be rude or tactless Manipulates people Demanding of others End justifies the means Work may become his god Demands loyalty in the ranks	Not people oriented Depressed over imperfections Chooses difficult work Hesitant to start projects Spends too much time planning Prefers analysis to work Self-deprecating Hard to please Standards often too high Deep need for approval	Not goal oriented Lacks self-motivation Hard to get moving Resents being pushed Lazy and careless Discourages others Would rather watch
F R I E N D S	Hates to be alone Needs to be center stage Wants to be popular Looks for credit Dominates conversations Interrupts and doesn't listen Answers for others Fickle and forgetful Makes excuses Repeats stories	Tends to use people Dominates others Decides for others Knows everything Can do everything better Is too independent Possessive of friends and mate Can't say, "I'm sorry" May be right, but unpopular	Lives through others Insecure socially Withdrawn and remote Critical of others Holds back affection Dislikes those in opposition Suspicious of people Antagonistic and vengeful Unforgiving Full of contradictions Skeptical of compliments	Dampens enthusiasm Stays uninvolved Is not exciting Indifferent to plans Judges others Sarcastic and teasing Resists change

Reprinted by permission from AFTER EVERY WEDDING COMES A MARRIAGE, Florence Littauer, Harvest House Publishers, All rights reserved.

Understanding Your Personality Profile Scores

Having transferred your checked words from the "Profile" pages 90-91 to the scoring sheet on pages 92-93, you should now have a pattern of your personality. Be sure to subtotal each column separately for strengths and for weaknesses.

Normal Healthy Patterns

Natural combinations of birth personalities are: Sanguine/Choleric; Phlegmatic/Sanguine; Choleric/Melancholy; Melancholy/Phlegmatic. One of the two will be your dominant and the other will be your secondary. Most everyone has a dominant and a secondary, but the numbers may vary greatly. For example 32 Choleric, with 8 Melancholy would be described as a very strong Choleric with some Melancholy traits.

However, it is also quite possible to have more evenly balanced scores in two columns. One or two checks in the remaining two columns can generally be ignored as insignificant. Any test such as this can be assumed to have a ten percent margin of error, for the words simply represent how you perceive yourself. Normal healthy patterns are usually characterized by similar and balancing scores of strengths and weaknesses in any single column.

Unnatural Combinations

There are two combinations, though often seen, that are not natural: 1: Sanguine/Melancholy, and 2. Choleric/Phlegmatic. Either of these two appearing on the scoring sheet in significant numbers is evidence of a "personality mask" as they are diametrically opposite and are not natural birth personality combinations. They are inevitably (1) the result of outside forces working in our lives to make us conform to someone else's concept of who we should be or (2) put on in childhood to survive in a difficult or dysfunctional family living situation.

Causes of masking include: domineering or alcoholic parent in childhood, strong rejection feelings, or emotional or physical abuse in childhood, childhood sexual interference or violation, single parent home, birth order, legalistic religious home, domineering and controlling spouse in adult life, adult abuse or rejection ion marriage.

Resources for Further Study

1. To Understand Personality Strengths and Weakness, **Personality Plus,** Florence Littauer, Fleming H. Revell Co.
2. To Understand Masking: **Your Personality Tree,** Florence Littauer, Word Books.
3. To Understand Effects of Childhood Trauma: **Freeing Your Mind from Memories that Bind.** Fred & Florence Littauer, and **The Promise of Restoration,** Fred Littauer, Thomas Nelson Publishers.
4. To Understand Children's Personalities: **Raising Christians, Not Just Children,** Florence Littauer, Word Books.
5. To Understand Your Leadership Potential, **Personalities in Power,** Florence Littauer, Huntington House.
6. To Understand Personalities in The Workplace, **Personality Puzzle,** Florence Littauer & Marita Littauer, Fleming H. Revell Co.

These invaluable books are available at your Christian bookstore, or can be ordered direct by calling CLASS Book Service, 1-800-433-6633.

Health and Fitness

6

Health and Fitness

Wellness is not just the absence of disease.
Wellness is optimal health. It is the maintenance and promotion of
one's health and physical well-being.

Entering college as either Freshmen or re-entry students is a time of change and challenge. If you now live in a dorm, or in an apartment with other students, your lifestyle has drastically changed. No longer does Mom prepare your breakfast or make sure you eat those vegetables. Now it's all up to you. You are in charge.

This chapter offers tips on how to be the best that you can be in regards to your overall health. Do you consider yourself to be healthy? Healthy is more than the lack of disease. Healthy means that you have optimal strength, energy and vitality.

✔ You are energized.

✔ You can perform.

✔ You are at your peak.

✔ You're the best that you can be.

I. WELLNESS IS IN . . . . SICKNESS IS OUT

Health and wellness is the name of the game in the 90's. Magazines and television programs bombard us with information about vitality, fitness and wellness. There's a spa on every corner. We all have access to what the health authorities are saying about health and wellness. We know that diet and exercise level are two lifestyle components that are crucial to "wellness."

Thirty percent of Americans are over-fat. Eighty percent of Americans do not exercise regularly. Only twenty percent exercise at least twenty minutes a day, three times a week.

Our exercise level has decreased since the year 1900. Our forefathers were farmers who worked with their hands and their bodies to make a living. Today our exercise is decreasing, and our fat is increasing. Americans consume about 40% percent of their diet in fat.

You don't have to be a part of that majority who eat too much and do not exercise—that majority who invite health problems because of their lifestyle. You can be in charge of your own destiny if you are willing to make a commitment to your health and to your lifestyle.

II. BALANCE AND WHOLENESS

Wellness refers to the wholeness of our bodies, our total well-being. Wellness is more than just physical. It includes the mental, the emotional and the physical aspects of each of us. Everything interrelates—mind, body and spirit—all need to be in unity.

For example, if we are over-stressed, we may experience stomach upsets or headaches. It is to our benefit if we can keep everything in balance or unity.

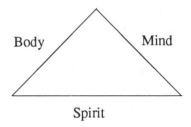

Part of that balance is the spiritual aspect; it is important to have a belief system. Having positive relationships is part of that balance. We also need to stay in the mainstream, maintain an active lifestyle, and remain involved with the people around us.

Consider yourself. Would you say that the physical, mental and emotional aspects of your life are in balance? If something is out of balance, it's your responsibility to re-focus and come back into balance.

III. CHECKLIST

The following lifestyle and wellness checklist can help you to determine your level of health and wellness.

1. Are you a nonsmoker? Smoking is the number one cause for disease today. 390,000 Americans will die this year because they have chosen to smoke.

They will die of cancer, stroke, lung disease, or heart disease.

2. Poor diet is the number two reason for disease. We're bombarded with diet information daily: Have a heart-healthy diet. Eat right. Low fats. More fiber. It is scientifically true that having a good diet can help prevent disease.

3. Exercise. *Physician and Sports Medicine Journal,* June 1991, said that inactive, sedentary people, "couch potatoes" who just sit around—are almost as great a risk for disease as people who smoke a pack of cigarettes a day. You can make a substantial difference in your overall wellness by incorporating exercise into your lifestyle.

4. Stress Management. The everyday U.S.A. lifestyle in the 90's incorporates a great deal of stress. We experience stress with our jobs, our school work, and with all that we are called upon to do. It is important to learn to manage stress. We need to find positive ways to get away from stress build-up which can cause disease. Many people who are under stress will suffer with chest palpitations, headaches, upset stomachs, and other problems. We need to include time for rest and recreation. We need time to let down and relax.

Some stress is good. It is a positive force in our lives, and can keep us going. But if we're constantly under stress and never have that time to let down, then we're headed for physiological problems. So take that time off. But stay in balance. When you're a college student, make sure there's not too much rest and relaxation.

5. Alcohol consumption is disastrous to your health. People who are influenced by too much alcohol will have health problems. They also are at risk for auto accidents, which result in injury and death.

6. Drugs. Stay away from drugs. We hear this from elementary school on: *Be smart. Say no. Cocaine can kill. One dose can kill.* The strain of marijuana today is higher than ever. So the results of using marijuana can be significant to your health. Avoid it.

7. Wear seat belts. That's simple, but it's important for a healthy lifestyle. Statistics prove that wearing seat belts saves lives.

How did you measure up? Would you rate your lifestyle excellent, good, fair, or poor? Could you make improvements? Remember, you are in charge of your own destiny. It's up to you. Nobody else is going to take care of you but yourself.

IV. LIFESTYLE

Lifestyle is the most critical risk factor related to disease, and it is one thing that you can be in charge of. You can't be in charge of your genes or your hereditary factor—your parents gave you that.

After lifestyle comes environment and medical care system, and then heredity, where you have no control. We can be in charge of most of the factors in regards to our overall health.

V. HOLISTIC APPROACH

Most centers for sports medicine take a holistic approach to wellness. They focus on prevention. Clients at centers for sports medicine receive not only a complete medical-physical, but they are also evaluated in regard to the impact their lifestyle has on their overall health.

Do the clients smoke? Do they exercise? How is their nutrition? Do they wear seat belts? All of these factors are incorporated in a wellness evaluation.

At sports medicine centers, clients undergo a complete fitness evaluation. This includes: muscular strength and endurance—how many push-ups and sit-ups can they do? How strong are they? How long can they go aerobically? The focus is on prevention.

Know your numbers. Pay attention when you have a medical check-up. Know your numbers. What is your blood pressure? your cholesterol? your HDL? your resting heart rate? Know all facets of yourself. Stay in charge. Take responsibility for your health.

Many people wait until it's too late. They drag an almost dead body to the doctor and say, "Fix me up. Do something for me." Sometimes it's just beyond any help.

Wellness, or a holistic approach, should be ongoing. It should be a lifetime pursuit. Wellness isn't something you practice for a year or two. You start now, and continue for the rest of your life.

Stay in control. Be aware of that triangle, that balance of mind, body, and spirit. They are connected. When you're out of focus and you're having problems, get help. There are people and programs at your university to help you get through this first tough semester. You are experiencing changes in study habits, and your work level and stress level are probably going up. Take advantage of the programs your university provides that help you orient yourself to a new lifestyle.

VI. DIET

When it comes to diet, the choices can be confusing. Pick up any magazine or newspaper, and you'll find these headlines jumping out at you:

- ✔ Get the fat out.
- ✔ Three Meals that Heal.
- ✔ Light Junk Food.
- ✔ Ten Vegetables That Will Heal.
- ✔ Eat six times a day and lose weight.
- ✔ This is the key to losing weight!
- ✔ Lose 10, 20, even 50 pounds!
- ✔ Turn your body into a super fat-burning machine.
- ✔ Totally destroys fat. Lose up to seven pounds in two days.

✔ See the pounds disappear daily.

✔ Take a pill—only $19.95 and fat disappears.

Don't we wish! Realistically, the only one way to take care of the fat in our diet and in our bodies is to watch our diet and to exercise.

VII. NUTRITION

All health-enthusiasts believe that as far as nutrition, you certainly are what you eat. If you eat over-fat, you will be over-fat. You become a product of what you eat.

You can determine your future by what you put into your mouth. The single, most-effective prevention for many diseases is a healthful diet. The benefits of a more nutritious and healthful diet are fewer health problems, better quality of life, and longer life.

Eat a balanced diet. Most of us have been taught in elementary school and on up to eat a balanced diet. Let's define a balanced diet. Carbohydrates should be 60% of your daily food intake. Protein should be only 10-15%, and fats should be less than 30%. The average American takes in 40% fat; we want to keep fat well below 30%. Hoburt Bailey, a health enthusiast and author of *The Target Diet,* says "Decrease your sugar, decrease your fat, and increase your fiber." That's basically what you need to do. Sounds pretty easy.

Drink plenty of water. Drink eight to ten glasses of water a day. Our bodies are mostly made up of water. We need to keep replenishing it. So carry it with you.

Count calories: Depending on individual size and metabolism, women need at least twelve to fifteen hundred calories per day; men need two to three thousand.

Think of yourself as a sleek Porsche automobile. Would you run it with diesel fuel? Or would you use good, high-test fuel? You would put in the best possible fuel, wouldn't you? Do the same for yourself.

VIII. WHAT DO WE EAT?

First, let's look at breakfast. Yes, you should eat breakfast. It's important to consistently take in the nutrients that our bodies need. People who only eat one meal a day cannot pack in the needed nutrients. Also, people who just eat the evening meal are almost certain to over-indulge. And their choices probably won't be good, because they will be so hungry, they will eat anything.

When considering breakfast, keep in mind that we want low fat, low sugar, but high fiber. That eliminates Twinkies or donuts. For an inexpensive, easy breakfast, try one cup of skim milk, half a cup of oatmeal, and microwave five minutes. Not only do you have high fiber, low sugar (or no sugar), and low fat, but you also get something that sticks with you. This simple, high carbohydrate breakfast will give you energy.

Carbohydrates are glycogens for the muscles, glycogens for the brain, glycogens for the nerves.

Eat like a "Bushman." Keep your eating habits simple. GrapeNuts are good. Read the label: Wheat, malted barley, salt and yeast—no preservatives.

If you need a fortified cereal, Total is good—either corn or whole grain. Fruit is always a good choice, because you get low sugar, low fat, and high fiber. It's good to keep fruit and vegetables on hand.

Lunch time—and you're starving. You want something that will fill you up and still be nutritious. Also if you're on campus, you may not have much time between classes. A good choice is a bagel and some fruit. You can brown bag that easily, and you will have good nutrients to get you through the day.

Bread is good—it's the staff of life. Choose whole grain bread, and don't smear it with butter. Keep it light with some low-fat margarine. Fresh fruits or vegetables are good choices for lunch.

What's for dinner? Because we want a diet high in carbohydrates, pasta is important. You can eat every kind of pasta imaginable; just watch what you put on it. Use a light spaghetti sauce—keep the meat low. Spaghetti, noodles, and other pastas give you good carbohydrates and low fat. Pasta is good fuel, it sticks with you, and it's easy to prepare. You can cook spaghetti in about ten minutes, add a little spaghetti sauce, a big salad, fresh vegetables, fruit, and maybe a whole-grain muffin. You can eat a lot and keep it low in fat when you're eating carbohydrates.

Beans are another important source of carbohydrate. Cook a pot of your favorite beans. If you have a crock pot, you can put them on in the morning and they will be ready to eat for dinner. You can also buy a wide variety of canned beans. Refried beans is a simple meal for college students who do their own cooking. Buy the vegetarian brand because they're made without lard. Refried beans are low-fat and a good source of carbohydrates. Lentils are also a good choice.

Potatoes are another good carbohydrate. Bake them in a few minutes in the microwave and they are ready to eat. Keep it light with the sauce or margarine—don't pile on the sour cream. Use a small amount of light margarine. Put a lot of vegetables on it. Try a cottage cheese puree with onions.

Don't forget rice. Brown rice has more nutrients than white rice because bleaching removes a lot of nutrients.

Snacks: Triscuits are whole-wheat, low-fat and low-salt. They have approximately 30% fat.

Many crackers are notorious for having as much as 50% fat. Just put a Ritz Cracker on a napkin and watch it soak up the oil.

Another good choice to keep around is Wasa Toasted Wheat Crisp Bread— only one gram of fat. Graham Crackers are a good choice—they are a little bit sweet and have about 30% fat.

Pretzels have very little fat, and you can buy either salted or unsalted. If you must have something sweet, try animal crackers; they are under 30% fat. Popcorn is a great snack. Just don't put all the oil and butter on it.

IX. LEARN TO READ LABELS

Since many of you now do your own grocery shopping, you need to be aware of what a label tells you. Most labels today will give you the contents in regards to a serving size, and break it down into calories, proteins, carbohydrates and fats.

You especially want to look at the percentage of fat, which is given in grams. For every gram of fat, there are nine calories. Let's say you have four crackers per serving, at 152 calories per serving; you have four grams of protein, sixteen of carbohydrates, and eight of fat. Multiply the eight grams of fat by nine to get a total of 72 calories coming from fat. Then divide 72 by 152, and you see that these crackers are almost 50% fat.

Check your labels when you go to the grocery store. You are in charge. Figure out the percentage of fat. Be aware that some of labels are misleading. They might say, "97% fat-free," but that figure could be based on the package weight. Figure the fat percentage for yourself. It may be a lot higher than what you would think.

X. EXERCISE

*Exercise and diet go together
in a healthy lifestyle.*

While it's good to take part in an aerobic class or work out in a fitness center, you don't need a complete fitness center to get fit. You just need to put on some good shoes and go for a twenty to thirty minute brisk walk three times a week.

Components of fitness. Aerobic capacity is probably the most important component of fitness. Physiologists know that when you exercise and get your heart rate up to a particular level, you are doing excellent things for your cardio-respiratory system.

But there are other aspects to fitness. If you just do aerobics, you're missing out on muscular-skeletal fitness, which includes strength, endurance, and flexibility.

How many push-ups can you do? How many sit-ups? Standards are established for how many both males and females should be able to do. Sit-ups increase abdominal strength, which is important for your lower back, as well as for the way you look.

Flexibility. How far can you stretch? Women generally are attached a little looser than men. But both want to be as flexible as possible. If you're really tight in the ham-strings, that can create problems with your back. And eight out of ten Americans suffer from back problems sometime in their lives.

Body composition. Body fat is determined with a measuring device called a caliper, and then computing the percentage of body fat. In terms of body composition, a female's percentage of body fat should be 25% or under to be "heart healthy." To be a "lean machine," the percentage would be 20%.

Males tend to have less body fat; they have more muscle. "Heart- healthy" for males would be about 15%; and 10-12% to be lean. Most professional basketball players measure 7 or 8% body fat.

Frequency. You should exercise at least three to five times a week—maybe six. While some people exercise every day, the body usually needs at least a day of rest.

Intensity. Physiologists have determined that your target zone for intensity is between 60 and 90% of your max heart-rate. A max heart-rate is 220 minus your age. Therefore, if you are 20, your max heart rate will be 200. 60% would be 120 heart beats per minute; 90% would be 180 beats. Walking will be about 60%. Running or doing high-impact aerobics will be 90%.

Time. The minimum amount of time to exercise is fifteen to twenty minutes. While a few endurance runners can go for hours, most people give out after a half hour or fifty minutes.

Types of exercise. Everything is available to us today: Tread mills, stair masters, life cycles—all are good if you need to be inside. There are many competitive sports, intramurals, health clubs, walking, running, jogging, skiing, swimming—the possibilities are endless. And once you're fit, you can participate in almost any activity. Even if you only ski once a year, you can always be ready if you maintain a fitness level.

Muscular strength and endurance are important. To build strength, you need heavy weights and few repetitions. For endurance, you need light weights and more repetitions.

Flexibility. Stretching should be done at least three times per week, but preferably daily. The intensity of the stretch should be to mild discomfort—you don't want any pain or pulled muscles. Maintain a range of motion to prevent injury. Each stretch should be for approximately fifteen to thirty seconds.

Benefits of Exercise

✔ burns calories

✔ improves cardiovascular system

✔ improves resting heart rate

✔ improves blood pressure

✔ improves cholesterol

✔ relieves stress

✔ renews and re-energizes us

✔ metabolic rate goes up

✔ appetite goes down

✔ heart rate down

✔ glucose tolerance up

✔ anxiety down

✔ depression down

✔ self-esteem up

✔ general well-being

Chapter Six

Discussion Questions and Exercises

To discover how well you take care of the different aspects of your health, complete the following sentences.

Exercise

1. This is the way I usually exercise:

_____

_____

_____

2. As a result of my physical conditioning, I look

_____

_____

_____

3. And I feel

_____

_____

_____

4. It would be easier for me to exercise regularly if I

_____

_____

_____

_____

5. I will try to stick to this exercise regimen:

_____

_____

_____

_____

_____

_____

Eating

1. My normal pattern of eating and drinking is:

_____

_____

_____

_____

_____

_____

2. Based on my calculation, my daily intake of calories in each category below is approximately:

   Carbohydrates: _____
   Protein: _____
   Fat: _____
   For a total of _____

3. Compared to the information in this chapter, I would say that my diet is

   ☐ Poor
   ☐ Fair
   ☐ Good
   ☐ Excellent

4. The things I would like to change most about my diet are:

    a. _____

    b. _____

    c. _____

Sleep

1. The number of hours I sleep each night is _____

2. On weekends, I normally sleep _____

3. I have trouble sleeping when _____

_____

_____

_____

4. The quality of my sleep is usually _____

_____

_____

_____

General Health

1. What concerns me more than anything about my health is: _____

_____

_____

_____

_____

_____

Nutrition Assessment

Baked Goods		Your Points	Total
Pies, cakes, cookies, sweet rolls, doughnuts	• I eat them 4 or more times a week. • I eat them 2-4 times a week. • I seldom eat baked good, or eat only low-fat baked goods.	0 1 2	
Poultry & Fish			
Chicken, turkey, seafood, tuna, etc.	• I rarely or never eat these foods. • I eat them 1-2 times a week. • I eat them 3 or more times a week.	0 1 2	
High-Fat Meat			
Luncheon meats, bacon, hot dogs, sausage, steak, regular & lean ground beef	• I eat high fat meats daily. • I eat high fat meats 3-4 times a week. • I rarely eat high fat meat. • I don't eat meat.	0 1 2 2	
Low-Fat Meat			
Extra lean hamburger, round steak, porkloin, roast, tenderloin, chuck roast	• I rarely eat lean meats. • I eat lean meats occasionally. • I eat mostly fat-trimmed lean red meats. • I don't eat meat.	0 1 2 2	
Cured & Smoked Meat & Fish			
Luncheon meats, hot dogs, bacon, ham & other smoked or pickled meats and fish	• I eat these foods 4 or more times a week. • I eat some 1-3 times a week. • I seldom eat these foods. • I don't eat meat or fish.	0 1 2 2	
Legumes			
Dried beans & peas (kidney, navy, lima, pinto, garbanzo, split-pea, lentil)	• I eat legumes less than once a week. • I eat these foods 1-2 times a week. • I eat them 3 or more times a week.	0 1 2	
Snacks			
Potato/corn chips, nuts, buttered popcorn, candy bars	• I eat these every day. • I eat some occasionally. • I seldom or never eat snacks.	0 1 2	
Dairy Products			
• I drink whole milk or 2% milk. • I drink nonfat or 1% milk.		0 1	
• I eat ice cream almost every day. • Instead of ice cream I eat ice milk, low-fat frozen yogurt, or sherbet. • I eat only fruit ices, and seldom eat frozen dairy desserts.		0 1 2	
• I eat mostly high-fat cheese (jack, cheddar, colby, Swiss, cream). • I eat both low- and high-fat cheeses. • I eat mostly low-fat cheeses (pot, 2% cottage, skim milk, mozzarella). • I don't eat cheese.		0 1 2 2	

Nutrition Assessment (continued)

Oils & Fats		Your Points	Total
Butter, margarine, shortening, mayonnaise, sour cream, lard, oil, salad dressing	• I always add these to foods in cooking and/or at the table. • I occasionally add these to foods in cooking or at the table. • I rarely add these to foods in cooking and/or at the table.	0 1 2	
	• I eat fried foods 3 or more times a week. • I eat fried foods 1-2 times a week. • I rarely or never eat fried foods.	0 1 2	
Whole Grains & Cereals			
Whole grain breads, brown rice, pasta, whole grain cereals	• I seldom each such foods. • I eat them 2-3 times a day. • I eat them 4 or more times a day.	0 1 2	
Vitamin C-Rich Fruits & Vegetables			
Citrus fruits and juices, green pepper, strawberries, tomatoes	• I seldom eat such foods. • I eat them 3-5 times a week. • I eat them daily.	0 1 2	
Deep Green / Deep Yellow Fruits & Vegetables			
Lettuce, spinach, squash, pumpkin, carrots, peaches	• I seldom eat them. • I eat them 1-2 times a week. • I eat them daily.	0 1 2	
Vegetables of the Cabbage Family			
Broccoli, cabbage, brussel sprouts, cauliflower	• I seldom eat them. • I eat them 1-2 times a week. • I eat them 3-4 times a week.	0 1 2	
Alcohol			
	• I have more than 2 drinks a day. • I drink alcohol every week, but not daily. • I occasionally or never drink alcohol.	0 1 2	
Personal Weight			
	• I'm more than 20 lbs. over my ideal weight. • I'm 10-20 lbs. over my ideal weight. • I'm within 10 lbs. of my ideal weight.	0 1 2	
Score		**Total Points**	

(0-12) A Warning
   Your diet is probably too high in fat, and too low in fiber-rich foods.
(13-17) Not Bad
   You still have a way to go.
(18+) You're Eating Smart
   You have been careful to limit your fats, and to eat a varied diet.

Source: Adapted from American Cancer Society Materials

♥ ♥ ♥

Scripture and Prayer

Do you not know that your body is a temple of the Holy Spirit, who is in you, whom you have received from God? You are not your own; you were bought at a price. Therefore honor God with your body." 1 Corinthians 6:19, 20 (NIV)

Heavenly Father,

I know that it's important for me to stay healthy and fit so that I can function at peak performance in my college career. Help me to do the things that contribute to a healthy, energized lifestyle. And help me to avoid those things that would endanger my health and could even prevent me from obtaining my goal of a college degree.

I also know that I'm going to be extremely busy and that the temptation will be great to skip meals, eat too much junk food, not exercise, and not get enough sleep. Help me to overcome those temptations and find creative ways to care for my physical, mental, emotional, and spiritual well-being.

Thank you that you have promised to meet all my needs—and that includes the need for nutritious food, exercise, and rest.

amen

Chapter Seven

Effective Communication

7

Effective Communication

Communication skill is one of the biggest factors of success.

When it comes to communication your perception might not be the same as someone else's. A major hindrance to effective communication is to assume that other people have the same perception that we do.

I. WHAT COMMUNICATION INVOLVES

Communication involves a transmitter, a receiver, and a message.

Usually that message is information. But it is something more—it is also you. You communicate "you." You and I communicate our very selves. The message transmitted is a mingling of infor-

mation and "you." Thus, the receiver of the message gets more than facts, information and opinions; the receiver also gets desires, feelings, and thoughts.

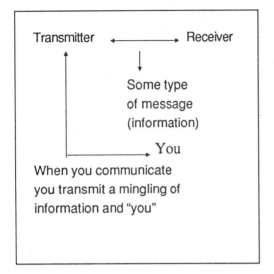

Transmitter ◄─────► Receiver
│
Some type
of message
(information)

You

When you communicate
you transmit a mingling of
information and "you"

communicate only on a basic level. But humans communicate so much. The pinnacle of life is very much related to communication; conversely, so are the lowest levels. Communication gives us the potential for either wonderful things or terrible things.

II. Communication Theory

Environment is important and greatly contributes to the quality of communication. Make sure you are close enough. Make sure the noise level is down.

In the classroom both the professor (transmitter) and the students (receivers) contribute to effective communication. Ideally the professor should stand or sit near enough to the students so he is easily heard. The students, for their part, should listen attentively and try not to make distracting sounds: whispering, scooting chairs, crackling paper.

Communication involves who you are as well as what you are saying—whether you are with a professor, a peer, a friend, or the Lord,

Many people, including business people and philosophers, believe that communication skill is one of the biggest factors of success. While it's important to get good grades in school, it takes more than knowledge to be successful in your chosen field. You must also be able to communicate that knowledge.

- ✔ Can you communicate with people?
- ✔ Can you communicate information clearly and concisely?
- ✔ Can you communicate a self—a being—that is conducive to the environment?

Communication is crucial. Communication is bound up with the essence of what it is to be a human being. Trees do not communicate. Cats and dogs

On the social scene, communication is also vital. Let's say that your girlfriend is talking to you while you are watching

118

a basketball game. Such an environment is not conducive to good communication. In order to have good, clear communication, there must be a minimization of noise.

III. PSYCHOLOGICAL PERSPECTIVE ON NOISE

Problems in communication occur when there is some type of "noise" between the sender and receiver.

Let me give you a psychological perspective on noise. "Noise" is not just from outside sources like radios, television, people talking, or traffic sounds. The "noise" that distracts from effective communication is in you—in your mind, your body, and your emotions. Messages, both verbal and non-verbal, are constantly coming to you. Psychologists think of this in terms of your having a sensory register. For ex-

ample, just sitting in class, you get sensory input from the pressure of the chair on your seat. But you do not focus on it until someone calls it to your attention. You get sensory input from inside your body. You get input from something that was said just a few minutes ago. You may even get input from some things in the future.

However, as a human, you also have a psychological perspective—we could call that a "filter." And what you let into your consciousness depends on the kind of filter you have. What is the filter? It's you. The filter includes your thoughts, your expectations, your opinions, your experiences, your fears, and your emotions—both good and bad. Thus, each person's filter will be different to varying degrees.

The information, or message, passes through your filter into what

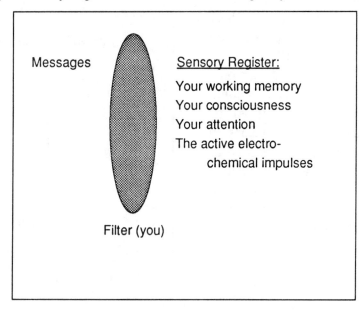

Messages

Sensory Register:

Your working memory
Your consciousness
Your attention
The active electro-
    chemical impulses

Filter (you)

psychologists describe as your working memory, or we could call it your consciousness—or your attention. Another name would be the active electrochemical impulses; this is information that is actively being charged through the senses.

It is possible for two people to hear exactly the same words, but one person will get a vastly different meaning from the other. Studies have been done that clearly demonstrate how people hear vastly different things—dependent on who they are, what they filter in, and who they are listening to. A person's "filter" will be different when listening to a girlfriend on a date than it will be when listening to a professor in class. In fact, the filter of what goes into your working memory or your consciousness may not be the same thing as what you're thinking at all. Somehow, there is some "noise" in your communication.

1. Recommendations for minimization of noise

Effective communication and success are closely tied. To be a successful teacher, lawyer, minister, wife or husband very much depends on communication. Effective communication, or the lack of it, also depends on your standards. In the following chart we see the standards that go into good communication as well as the ones that result in bad communication.

Taking time is a standard of good communication. Whether you are attempting to communicate with your teacher, your peer, or someone at the store or the job, take time. Take time with that person.

Failing to take time results in poor communication. We say, "Sorry God, no time for you today." Or, "Sorry friend,

Communication	
Good	Bad
Take time	No time
Listen\attend	Ignore
Toward harmony	Contrary
Caring	Selfish

no time. I have to do lots of things. I have to study and write a paper, clean the house, mow the yard, go to the store." Or, "Sorry boyfriend, I have to do all these other things that leave me no time for you."

Listen, or we could say "attend." In a user's computer analogy, we would say "executive monitoring." Or a psychological term would be your *metacognition.* Those terms simply mean that you are watching what you are doing all the time. You are watching your thoughts, and you are paying attention in a conversation. And if you have good standards that are focused on listening and attending, a certain perception activates another perception, which at that moment is your reference point for the incoming information.

The opposite of listening would be ignoring. For example, when in class, if your standards include a dislike for a certain professor, and you sit there mentally criticizing her, the information that professor is transmitting will be filtered through your dislike. Communication, in this case, will be poor. Your dislike becomes the "noise" that hinders effective communication.

But if your standards are such that a person is the most wonderful in the world, you will do those things that make for good communication. You will take time. You will listen. You will pay attention.

Toward harmony. If desiring harmony is a standard in you, then even in the midst of disagreement about the information, there will be some type of harmony between the two of you.

The opposite is toward disharmony or contrariness. For example, you talk to some people and everything is contrary—everything is opposite. In those cases when you disagree, what you're putting paramount in you is information and ideas rather than hearts.

Caring. For good communication, even if you're involved in a big time business deal, there will be some caring—caring about the situation and the other person. The other side—the bad side—is selfish. If you are only interested in what you want or in having your needs met, you will project that attitude along with any information you are giving. Also, you will filter any input from the other party through your selfish desires and motives. The result—extremely poor communication.

All of the attitudes listed under bad communication: no time, ignore, contrary, and selfish are types of "noise" that hinder effective communication.

You can learn to discern where "noise" hinders your communication in the classroom. Is it something in your thinking that causes you not to comprehend what the professor is teaching?

Where are communication problems occurring when you are with an employer? Or with a friend? You can be with friends, out having a good time when there is some kind of misunderstanding as a result of poor communication.

Bad attitudes and bad standards are a source of the problem of ineffective communication. But when we have good standards of taking time, listening, desiring harmony, and caring, the channels will be open and free from "noise" so that hearts, humans and information can flow between one another.

Tips on good classroom communication

Follow directions. One professor said that the single biggest hindrance to success in a student is failure to follow through on the directions on the syllabus.

Ask questions. Whether it is unclear communication on the part of the teacher, or unclear reception on your part, if you do not know what is required of you in class, ask your professor. Usually, professors like for students to ask, especially if there is genuine concern, and the student is not trying to show off. Also, professors generally like to see you after class, or like for you to come by the office, rather than have you interrupt class.

Watch your attitude around your teachers. Be careful what kind of attitude you communicate. Perhaps you are upset about something. Maybe you've just broken up with your

boyfriend. Maybe you've been out all weekend doing things you really shouldn't have been involved in, and you're filled with "grunge."

When we have bad attitudes, it's often because there has been some degree of "junk" in the last few days that has just become attached to us. Things happened that affected us adversely. When bad attitudes are present, don't communicate them to your professors. They are human too, and they will react to you. So guard your tongue, and you'll keep yourself from a lot of trouble.

Talk about the class content with some of your peers. This is more than just studying for a test. Talking over class content can help you apply and relate classroom knowledge to real life experience. One might call this "Superman student behavior," since Superman is one who excels to the heights.

V. THE MEANING OF LIFE

The meaning of life is very much related to communication. Genesis 1:26 gives us God's purpose in creating human beings. *"Then God said, 'Let Us make man in Our image, according to Our likeness....'"* God created man and woman to be in His image—to be like Him. He created "you" to be like Him.

When we consider God's purpose in creating us in respect to communication, we see that God wants senders and receivers who are like Him. God wants this for all of us.

Therefore, if we are created in God's image, and we want to understand the meaning of life, we need to know about God. On the chart below are some of the attributes that make up God's image, as well as those things that make up the image of the evil one. As you also can see on the chart, we are positioned in between.

God is Light. Have you ever sensed in your heart that there is light, that there is a brightness within? That light is of God, because He is light.

✔ God is Love.

✔ God is Kindness.

✔ God is Peace.

✔ God is Oneness.

Can you see some of these things related to communication? Good communication will reflect these qualities.

The other side of the chart lists characteristics of the evil one. Darkness is the first. Have you sometimes sensed darkness inside you? You might be shining

God's Image		Satan's image
Light	**Y**	Darkness
Love	**O**	Hate\ lust
Kindness	**U**	Selfishness
Peace		Strife

on the outside to people, but you know that inside there is something dark. Darkness is an image of the evil one coming through.

We have a choice whether we will allow the good image of God to be exhibited in our lives and in our communication with one another, or if we will succumb to the devil's attempts to influence us to project his ugly dark image.

God wanted you to be in His image—He created you for that purpose. But there's more to it than that. The other big part that most of us don't know that well, is He wanted us to be in His image **together—in communication.** The Bible speaks of *Koinonia* or fellowship; one translation for *Koinonia* is communication. What is the real fellowship and communication God desires? He wants us to communicate His image to one another. To communicate light, love, kindness, peace, and oneness. There is no "noise" in these kinds of communications.

What does the devil want for us? He wants darkness; the Bible says that the devil is the ruler of darkness. He wants our image to project his characteristics of hate, lust, selfishness, strife, and division. In very intricate, subtle ways, the devil wants to influence you so that your image is not God's, but the devil's.

When a human has good communication with another person—a professor, a peer, an acquaintance at the store—the essence of God is being transmitted.

Whether it is God Himself filling a person, or whether it is someone living by higher standards (which still come from God), in either case, when there is good communication, people are filled with the good qualities that are the image of God.

When there is bad communication in terms of dissatisfaction, or because the information gets clouded, the elements of darkness, hate, selfishness, strife and division are operative.

VI. WHAT THE BIBLE SAYS ABOUT COMMUNICATION

The Bible has much to say about how we should communicate with one another.

"If anyone among you thinks he is religious, and does not bridle his tongue but deceives his own heart, this one's religion is useless." James 1:26

"Let no corrupt communication proceed out of your mouth, but what is good for necessary edification, that it may impart grace to the hearers. And do not grieve the Holy Spirit of God, by whom you were sealed for the day of redemption. Let all bitterness, wrath, anger clamor, and evil speaking be put away from you, with all malice. And be kind to one another, tenderhearted, forgiving one another, just as God in Christ

also forgave you."
Ephesians 4:29—32

Notice that these verses all have to do with communication. When you're with others, can you communicate only that which edifies, or builds up, others, that which expresses caring and concern for them?

When biblical principles such as these guide your conduct, when you live in that realm, you will be happy, and you will be satisfied in the depths of your being. You also will have good communication and good relationships.

"Brood of vipers [little snakes that will bite you]! "How can you, being evil speak good things? For out of the abundance of the heart the mouth speaks. A good man out of the good treasure of his heart brings forth good things, and an evil man out of the evil treasure brings forth evil things. But I say to you that for ever idle word men may speak, they will give account of it in the day of judgment. For by your words you will be justified, and by your words you will be condemned."
Matthew 12:34—37

That's God's Word! It says that every idle word—words that are just in the realm of nowhere land—will be accounted for.

"But you are a chosen generation, a royal priesthood, a holy nation,

His own special people, that you may proclaim the praises of Him who called you out of darkness into His marvelous light."
I Peter 2:9

That's the gospel! It's not just going to heaven. The gospel is being called out of the darkness—out of living in the darkness—out of noisy communication—out of darkness into light. And God still calls you and me to live in the light and to communicate the qualities of light instead of the qualities darkness. Jesus said that we who believe in and accept Him are the light of the world, and that we are to let our light shine in a darkened world. One of the ways we let that light shine is through good communication.

Remember that Greek word, *Koinonia*, or fellowship, is properly translated "sharing one another, a joint participation," which means a sender and receiver with no noise.

*"The life was manifested, and we have seen, and bear witness, and **declare** to you that eternal life which was with the Father and was manifested to us—that which we have seen and heard we declare to you, that you also may have fellowship with us [genuine God fellowship with one another]; and truly our fellowship is with the Father and with His son Jesus Christ. And these things we write to you that your joy may*

be full. This is the message which we have heard from Him and declare to you, that God is light and in Him is no darkness at all. If we say that we have fellowship with Him, and walk in darkness, we lie and do not practice the truth. But if we walk in the light as He is in the light, we have fellowship with one another [genuine communication], and the blood of Jesus Christ His son cleanses us from all sin." I John 1:2-7

The Word of God is very clear: We may say that we have fellowship (good communication) with God, but if we are walking in the things of darkness, we lie and do not practice the truth.

We can deceive ourselves; our rational mind can say, "everything's okay." But the word of God is the plumb line—the absolute standard for truth.

Human communication at this level is the highest pinnacle possible—to share goodness with one another, to share our hearts with one another, having no "noise" between us is to be in the image of God. Remember, God created us in His image. And even humans without the Lord, the ones who are the most successful, strive for this high level of communication. And they attain it to some degree. They attain listening. They attain a oneness. They attain something of kindness.

However, without God no man or woman is truly satisfied in the real depths of their being. When we take God into our lives, we can communicate with Him every day. We can be filled with His presence, with His light, with His essence.

If you're a born again Christian, the Lord is in your heart all the time. And He's there, wanting to have some real, high quality communication. He will fill you with Himself, with the essence of who He is—His image. And you, as you walk in that light will communicate His image of love, kindness, peace and joy to a world that so desperately needs to come out of darkness and into light.

Chapter Seven

Discussion Questions and Exercise

1. There are things we think about telling people, but don't. Examine your relationships and complete the following statements.

    I realize that I am not communicating

    about _____

    with _____

    I realize that I am not communicating

    about _____

    with _____

    I realize that I am not communicating

    about _____

    with _____

    I realize that I am not communicating

    about _____

    with _____

    Choose one or two ideas from this chapter that can open communication with these people in these areas. Describe how you will use these ideas.

    I intend to ....

    _____

    _____

    _____

_____

_____

_____

2. Rate yourself on communication and relationships.

    5 points - This statement is always or almost always true of me.
    4 points - This statement is often true of me.
    3 points - This statement is sometimes true of me.
    2 points - This statement is seldom true of me.
    1 point - This statement is never or almost never true of me.

    1. _____ I have the ability to make friends and start new relationships.

    2. _____ I am open to being with people I don't especially like in order to help them or learn from them.

    3. _____ People tell me that I am a good listener.

    4. _____ I am candid with others about how I feel and what I want.

    5. _____ I can communicate an idea clearly and concisely.

    6. _____ I can communicate with the Lord anytime and anywhere.

    7. _____ I develop and maintain several supportive relationships.

    8. _____ I can communicate my concerns and frustrations without blaming others.

    Total points _____

3. Pick an issue that is currently bothering you, and write it here: _____

    _____

    _____

    _____

    _____

Then, pretend that you are talking to the person who is associated with the issue. List five possible "noises" that may hinder effective communication between you—the "transmitter" and the other person—the "receiver".

a. _____

b. _____

c. _____

d. _____

e. _____

With a conscious effort to eliminate these noises, paraphrase an effective message to raise the issue with this person.

_____

_____

_____

_____

_____

_____

_____

_____

_____

_____

_____

♥ ♥ ♥

Scripture and Prayer

A man finds joy in giving an apt reply—and how good is a timely word! Proverbs 15:23 NIV
A man of knowledge uses words with restraint....
Proverbs 17:27 NIV

Heavenly Father,

I ask you to help me become a more effective communicator—to become a better listener and a better transmitter. Help me to listen attentively and respectfully when I am in the classroom. And when I am called upon to answer a question in class, help me to remain calm so that I communicate clearly. Help me to develop good communication skills—such as, taking time, listening, and caring for others.

I thank you for Jesus—the greatest communicator of all. Help me to learn from his example of communicating truth in love, and of speaking appropriately to the great variety of people he met and taught.

amen

Choosing A Career
and A Major

8

Choosing A Career and A Major

Choosing work you enjoy is extremely important!
It is a pathway to success.

Author Peter Jenkins chose to do what he enjoyed, and it turned out to be the source of his success. When he graduated from college in the early 1970's, instead of going to work, he did something a little different. He was disenchanted with America because of the war situation and different concerns of the time. So he decided to take a walk across America and see what it was like.

First, he walked down the East Coast, through the Appalachian Mountains, and on to New Orleans. When he ran out of money along the way, he just stopped and found some kind of job. Usually, he also found a local family—it didn't matter what race—who would take him in. He made many friends and learned a lot about America. His faith in America was restored.

In the seventies and the early eighties he, and his wife later with him, published two books based on his experience: *Waltz Across America* and *The Walk West*. These books were extremely popular, and Peter Jenkins enjoyed success as a writer.

Doing what you enjoy—regardless of what it is—is a pathway to success. Peter Jenkins did not set out to be a writer when he began his walk across America. But his writing career was conceived in those early years.

I. CHOOSE WORK YOU ENJOY

If you are studying and working in a certain field and you don't like it, don't continue it next semester; take something else. There's no reason to be unhappy with your studies or your work.

You'll be more successful if you're happy. You also will have better health, because health is connected to happiness. The writer of the Book of Proverbs said: *A merry heart does good like medicine....* Proverbs 17:22

I. Choose a career—then a major.

Students often reverse this order. They choose a major first, assuming that somehow or other that will become their career. But choosing a career first will give much better direction.

II. HOW TO CHOOSE A CAREER

While several systems—some more complicated than others—can help in choosing a career, we're going to focus on a simple two-point system that has proved extremely helpful:

- ✔ Evaluate your interests.
- ✔ Analyze your abilities.

Evaluate your interests. What subjects appeal to you? What kind of work appeals to you? This gives you part of the answer. Next, what do you read in your spare time? What do you like to do in your leisure time? Is it music? sports? art? This gives added insight into your interests.

Analyze your abilities. What do you do best? If you can get a job in which you have both interest and abilities, you will not only be better satisfied but also you will be more productive.

Over your lifetime, you have developed and used a variety of skills and abilities. There is no such thing as a person with no ability. Part of a person's inherent design is the natural desire to frequently use specific abilities. Perhaps you know of a student who is "forever studying," or the next door neighbor who is always "skiing," or your friend "who just loves to cook." These are people who can't help but put their abilities to use.

What happens when you become like these folks, and get immersed in using your own skills? You notice that the time just flies! You are unconscious of the hour and wrapped up in the activity of the moment, because you are using the ability or abilities that motivate you the most. Such unbridled enthusiasm is a sure sign that you indeed excel in using the abilities that give you the greatest enjoyment.

1. Checklist

Use the following checklist to help you determine your best abilities. First, check the abilities that you think you presently have. Then, identify the five skills that you are most confident about. Circle those five skills.

___writing
___reporting information
___coming up with ideas
___applying technical knowledge
___explaining
___helping others
___scheduling
___problem solving
___keeping records
___reading
___being creative
___socializing
___negotiating
___selling
___handling money
___managing
___directing others
___making mechanical things
___encouraging
___conversing
___building things
___abstract thinking
___being adept with numbers
___entertaining
___public speaking
___planning
___taking risks
___being accurate
___other

Coupled with knowledge and experience, these dominant abilities form the foundation for your best accomplishments, including those you are bound to pursue throughout your career. After determining your interests and abilities, and considering the career options in that field, then you can select your major (Additional charts at end of chapter).

> *Choosing a career, establishing your major, and setting appropriate goals will help you to move ahead faster and smoother.*

Selecting a career that fits your interests and abilities will not only guide your major, but also your minor. It can even give you direction in choosing electives. Your career selection also can guide many of your outside activities—such as the type of part time or summer work you do.

To illustrate how interests can lead to a career choice, a professor told the following story about one of his students.

I first met Brenda when she was in high school and visited Grand Canyon University for a cadaver demonstration. Brenda entered college as a pre-nursing student. However, during the first year she decided to become a medical doctor. It is not unusual for that kind of change to happen along the way.

Brenda often came to my office to ask if she could borrow a particular book. She would pull down a thick, medical book from the shelf and say, "I just want to read a little bit here in the lobby." Sometimes Brenda would ask me what I had read recently, and if it was something medical, she would reply, "That sounds interesting. Maybe I ought to read that."

Brenda's spare time interests were varied, but a clue to her primary interest could be found in the type of work she selected to do during summer break. One summer she worked in the Heart Institute with Dr. Dietrich; two other summers she worked with plastic surgeons. Her interest in medicine was evident.

Brenda chose a Biology Major, a Chemistry Minor, and a Music Minor—music is a hobby. She had a double minor, and she planned to go on to medical school.

III. WHAT IF YOU'RE NOT SURE ABOUT A MAJOR?

Students are sometimes undecided about a career and a major—and that's all right. But it's better to go ahead and make a tentative choice and work in that direction. There is nothing wrong with changing later. A lot of people do. Interests change. New skills and abilities are acquired.

As your college years continue, if you feel the urge to change your initial interest of study, go ahead and do it. The main thing is to do what you enjoy.

It's important to choose a career that you want to do, that you enjoy doing. Many people return to college to get a degree in education or some other field after they have been in other careers.

In many cases, people give up good salaries in careers that are just draining them and come back to college to pursue what they really want to do. Often people come and say, "I knew I wanted to be a teacher a long time ago. I finally decided I'm going to do it."

*Whatever you do
in your career,
choose something
that you enjoy,
something that you really,
really like to do.*

IV. CHOOSE A CAREER WITH A HIGH DEMAND

If all other factors are equal, it's wise to choose a career with a high demand. For example, in the field of Biology, the high demand areas are in Medicine. And the strongest demands in Medicine are in Physical Therapy and Occupational Therapy. Other high demand fields are Pharmacology and Nursing.

If your field of study is business, there are probably areas that appeal to you more than others. Find out which of your strongest interests are in areas of high demand and concentrate on those areas.

Help in choosing a career is available from several sources. Your advisor, or other faculty members, can help you determine a career major. Career guidance books are available as well as other programs to help you rate yourself on a scale according to interests and ability. These resources can help you choose a career and give you information on different jobs in that field.

V. SEEK GOD'S LEADERSHIP

Seek God's leadership in choosing a career. God will not lead you into a career that you will hate. He is a wise, loving Heavenly Father, and He wants happy, cooperative workers in His kingdom. If you feel the Lord is leading you in an area in which you are not comfortable, or if you keep having that inner nudging to go in a direction other than what you've chosen, there are ways to determine the Lord's leading.

✔ Pray about the matter. Not just once or twice, but make this a priority prayer project.

✔ Talk with your advisors at school, your parents, your pastor, or a teacher at church or school.

✔ Ask God to give you a confirmation of this leading or "nudging." This could be in the form of an opportunity opening in that area; it might be something you read in the Bible that speaks personally to you. It might even be "putting out a fleece" like Gideon did in Judges Chapter Six. Or confirmation could also be a deep settled inner peace which tells you that this is the right thing for you to do.

✔ Most importantly: Give it time. Give God time. Give yourself time. He is never in as big a hurry as we are.

VI. BELIEF AND PERSISTENCE— TWO QUALITIES FOR SUCCESS

To illustrate two important qualities for success, a Professor told the following story about his dog, Ginger.

I was on the back porch of my home, preparing a lecture for class. Ginger was out in the yard, and she came prancing up to me with a rock in her mouth. We have a very rocky yard, so she brings them to me and I throw them off in the distance where she can't see them. Then she has a fine time running to find the rock.

On this particular day, Ginger brought a rock and dropped it on the ground beside my chair. I said, "Ginger, go away. I'm busy." A few minutes later, Ginger picked up the rock and dropped it on the chair beside me. Again I told her, "Go away. I'm busy." She nudged me with her nose, and once more I told her to go away.

Finally, Ginger took her big fat paw and began pawing me. How can you write when a dog is pawing you? So, I did what Ginger wanted. I picked up the rock and threw it. She ran off, wagging her tail, sniffing the ground. Ginger was a happy dog.

The moral of this story is that the determined dog gets her rock. Ginger *believed* that I would eventually throw the rock, and she *persisted* until I did.

We can get our "rocks" too. We can get what we want if we have the right determination and the right belief.

1. Belief

When you believe that you can get what you want, chances are, you will do more to get it than you would if you didn't believe it. Belief is extremely important.

If you find that you frequently say, "I can't do this," or "I can't do that," you need to make a change. You need to strike out the "T," changing can't to can.

- ✔ I can do it.
- ✔ I can do well with my studies.
- ✔ I can choose a good career.
- ✔ I can set goals that will allow me to get to that career.

Anytime you catch yourself slipping into a negative attitude about anything, repeat several times "I can. I can do it." Let that change your attitude from negative to positive.

Jesus said, *"...all things are possible to him who believes."* Mark 9:23. He didn't say "some things." He said "all things."

We all would have to admit that sometimes it is difficult to have faith that all things are possible if we believe. But the nearer we come to believing that, the better we will do in life.

The Apostle Paul said, *"I can do all things through Christ who strengthens me."* Philippians 4:13

Paul not only said that, he believed it, and look at his accomplishments! We still reap the benefits of them today.

It is amazing what can be accomplished if you believe that you can do all things through Christ who gives you strength.

2. Persistence

To your belief that you can do a thing, add the persistence to stay with it. That's what Ginger, the dog, did. She believed that her master would finally throw the rock if she persisted in her efforts.

Jesus illustrated the power of persistence with this story:

"Suppose you went to a friend's house at midnight, wanting to borrow three loaves of bread. You would shout up to him, 'A friend of mine has just arrived for a visit and I've nothing to give him to eat.' He would call down from his bedroom, 'Please don't ask me to get up. The door is locked for the night and we are all in bed. I just can't help you this time.' But I'll tell you this—though he won't do it as a friend, if you keep knocking long enough he will get up and give you everything you want— just because of your persistence. And so it is with prayer—keep on asking and you will keep on getting; keep on looking and you will keep on finding; knock and the door will be opened. Everyone who asks, receives; all who seek, find; and the door is opened to everyone who knocks."
Luke 11:5–10 (TLB)

Several highly successful men had the quality of persistence. Thomas Edison and Henry Ford were mentioned in a how-to-succeed book by Napolean Field who knew these men personally and studied them over a period of years. He said that he found no quality, save persistence, in either of them, that even remotely suggested the major source of their stupendous achievements.

Add belief and persistence to the other qualities mentioned in this book, and you will be on the road to success. These principles work equally for either individual success or group success.

✔ First: you need a vision— set your goal.

✔ Second: you need belief— believe that you can do it.

✔ Third: you need persistence— you have to work on it.

✔ The result is that you achieve what you set out to do, whether it is an individual goal or a group goal.

Somebody said that it couldn't be done.

But he with a chuckle replied,

That maybe it couldn't

But he would be one

Who wouldn't say so till he tried.

So he buckled right in

With a trace of a grin on his face.

If he worried, he hid it.

He started to sing

As he tackled the thing

That couldn't be done and he did it.

by Edgar Guess

The charts on this page and the next three can also help you to determine your interests and work preferences.

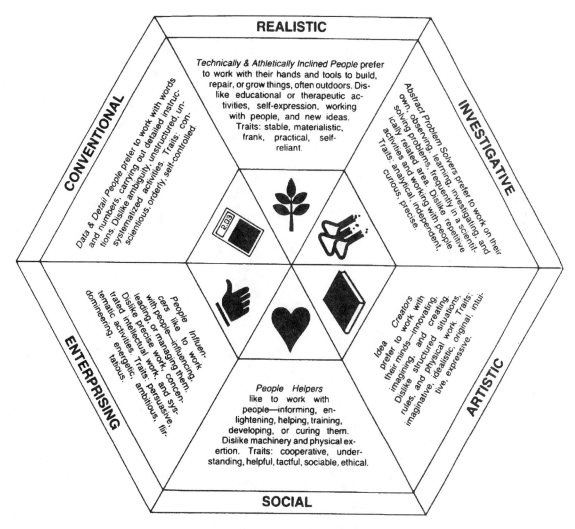

Figure 6. The Six Personality Types

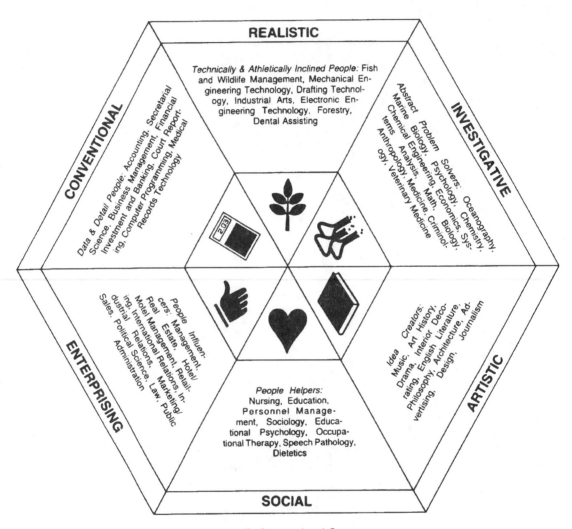

REALISTIC

Technically & Athletically Inclined People: Fish and Wildlife Management, Mechanical Engineering Technology, Drafting Technology, Industrial Arts, Electronic Engineering Technology, Forestry, Dental Assisting

CONVENTIONAL

Data & Detail People: Accounting, Secretarial Science, Business Management, Financial Investment and Banking, Court Reporting, Computer Programming, Medical Records Technology

INVESTIGATIVE

Abstract Problem Solvers: Oceanography, Marine Biology, Psychology, Chemistry, Chemical Engineering, Economics, Systems Analysis, Math, Biology, Anthropology, Medicine, Criminology, Veterinary Medicine

ENTERPRISING

People Influencers: Management, Hotel/Motel Management, Retailing, International Relations, Industrial Relations, Marketing/Sales, Political Science, Law, Public Administration, Real Estate

ARTISTIC

Idea Creators: Music, Art History, Drama, Interior Decorating, English Literature, Advertising, Design, Journalism, Philosophy, Architecture

SOCIAL

People Helpers: Nursing, Education, Personnel Management, Sociology, Educational Psychology, Occupational Therapy, Speech Pathology, Dietetics

Figure 7. Occupational Groups

142

Table 8. Comparison of the Personality Types

	Realistic	Investigative	Artistic
Characteristics	Stable Physical Practical Frank Self-reliant	Analytical Independent Curious Intellectual Precise	Imaginative Idealistic Original Expressive Impulsive
Likes	Outdoor work Mechanics Athletics Working with plants, tools, and animals	Abstract problems Science Investigation Unstructured situations Working alone	Ideas Self-expression Creativity Unstructured situations Working alone
Dislikes	Educational activities Self-expression Working with people	Repetitive activities Rules Working with people	Structure Rules Physical work Details Repetitive activities
Orientation	Hands-on activities	Problem solving	Idea creating
Preferred Skills	Building repairing Making and growing things	Problem solving Analytical reasoning Developing models and systems	Creating Visualizing Unstructured tasks Imagining
People Who Characterize the Styles	Thomas Edison The Wright Brothers Antonio Stradivari Chris Evert Lloyd Johannes Gutenberg Neil Armstrong Amelia Earhart	Albert Einstein Sherlock Holmes George Washington Carver Madam Curie Sigmund Freud Charles Darwin Admiral Grace Hopper	Alex Haley Beverly Sills Ludwig von Beethoven Michelangelo Buonarroti Wm. Shakespear Baryshnikov Emily Dickinson Frank Lloyd Wright

Table 8. (continued)

Social	Enterprising	Conventional
Cooperative	Persuasive	Conscientious
Understanding	Domineering	Orderly
Helpful	Energetic	Persistent
Tactful	Ambitious	Conforming
Sociable	Flirtatious	Efficient
People	Power	Order
Attention	People	Carrying out details
Discussion	Status	Organizing
Helping	Influencing	Structure
Socializing	Managing	Working with data
Physical work	Systematic activities	Unsystematized activities
Working with tools	Precise work	Lack of structure
Working outdoors	Concentrated intellectual work	Ambiguity
People assisting	People influencing	Detail & data
Interpersonal activities	Leading	Detailed tasks
Establishing rapport	Managing	Following directions
Communicating	Persuading	precisely
Helping	Motivating others	Repetitive tasks
Helen Keller	Henry Ford	E.F. Hutton
Joyce Brothers	Winston Churchill	Dr. Watson (Sherlock
Carl Menninger	Martin Luther King	Holmes' assistant)
Kenneth Clark	Margaret Thatcher	Noah Webster (dictionary)
Florence Nightingale	Lee Iacocca	Melvil Dewey (Dewey
Mother Teresa	Laura Ashley	decimal system)
Mahatma Gandhi	Golda Meir	Herman Hollerith
Albert Schweitzer		(keypunch card)
		Carolus Linnaeus (botanist)

Chapter Eight

Discussion Questions and Exercise

Interest and activity assessment

Like	**Dislike**
1–2 like a little	1–2 dislike a little
3–6 like considerably	3–6 dislike considerably
7–10 love it!	7–10 hate it!

Like   **Dislike**

☐_____   ☐_____   Designing my own computer program (I)

☐_____   ☐_____   Playing a musical instrument (A)

☐_____   ☐_____   Organizing a club, or conference (E)

☐_____   ☐_____   Writing a novel or a piece of music (A)

☐_____   ☐_____   Teaching games to children (S)

☐_____   ☐_____   Operating machinery or using hand tools (R)

☐_____   ☐_____   Serving on social events committee (S)

☐_____   ☐_____   Reading science magazines (I)

☐_____   ☐_____   Working in a garden (R)

☐_____   ☐_____   Keeping a detailed account of personal expenses (C)

☐_____   ☐_____   Playing Chess or doing crossword puzzle (I)

☐_____   ☐_____   Proofreading (C)

☐_____   ☐_____   Doing work with a microscope (I)

☐_____   ☐_____   Helping someone with a personal problem (S)

☐_____   ☐_____   Taking a course in psychology, religion, or sociology (S)

☐_____ ☐_____ Designing or testing out a model rocket (I)

☐_____ ☐_____ Engaging in political discussion (E)

☐_____ ☐_____ Getting acquainted with influential people (E)

☐_____ ☐_____ Acting in a play or musical (A)

☐_____ ☐_____ Taking a bookkeeping or accounting course (C)

☐_____ ☐_____ Coming up with new ideas for doing things (A)

☐_____ ☐_____ Taking a business, management or sales class (E)

☐_____ ☐_____ Meeting new people (S)

☐_____ ☐_____ Reading magazines like Popular Mechanics (R)

☐_____ ☐_____ Reading poetry, philosophy or fiction (A)

☐_____ ☐_____ Solving math of logic problem (I)

☐_____ ☐_____ Home repair like carpentry or plumbing (R)

☐_____ ☐_____ Working in a neat, organized structure setting (C)

☐_____ ☐_____ Keeping an accurate appointment book (C)

☐_____ ☐_____ Assisting a scouting or sports group (S)

Total:

      Like   Dislike

A _____

C _____

E _____

I _____

R _____

S _____

1. Do I have a narrow range of interest areas, or do I have a wide variety of interests?

   _____

   _____

   _____

   _____

   _____

2. What kinds of activities does my profile indicate I might enjoy spending more time doing?

   _____

   _____

   _____

   _____

   _____

3. Based on my interests and abilities, what are three possible careers I might choose? For each career, what are two majors I might be interested in?

Careers	Majors
A. _____	_____
	_____
B. _____	_____
	_____
C. _____	_____
	_____

Graduation Plan

Fall	Spring	Summer
_____	_____	_____
_____	_____	_____
_____	_____	_____
_____	_____	_____
_____	_____	_____
Fall	**Spring**	**Summer**
_____	_____	_____
_____	_____	_____
_____	_____	_____
_____	_____	_____
_____	_____	_____
Fall	**Spring**	**Summer**
_____	_____	_____
_____	_____	_____
_____	_____	_____
_____	_____	_____
_____	_____	_____
Fall	**Spring**	**Summer**
_____	_____	_____
_____	_____	_____
_____	_____	_____
_____	_____	_____
_____	_____	_____
Fall	**Spring**	**Summer**
_____	_____	_____
_____	_____	_____
_____	_____	_____
_____	_____	_____
_____	_____	_____

Building Blocks to Your Vocational Future

LONG TERM GOALS

Job title I aspire to:

(   )

Salary level I desire:

$_____

Values I need in my work environment:

1. _____
2. _____
3. _____

Environmental setting I most prefer to work in:	Geographical region I most prefer:
1._____	1._____
2._____	2._____
3._____	3._____

Types of . . . I most like to work with:

People	Information	Things
1. _____	1._____	1. _____
2. _____	2._____	2. _____
3. _____	3._____	3. _____

MY FOUNDATIONAL SKILL BASE
Specific skills I most like to utilize in working with:

People	Information	Things
1._____	1. _____	1. _____
2._____	2. _____	2. _____
3._____	3. _____	3. _____

♥ ♥ ♥

Scripture and Prayer

In his heart a man plans his course, but the Lord determines his steps. Proverbs 16:9 NIV
The wisdom of the prudent is to give thought to their ways.... Proverbs 14:8 NIV

Heavenly Father,

Thank you for the privilege of being able to choose a career and work toward that goal in the coming years. Help me to evaluate that choice (or make that choice), and become settled within myself that this is the right path for me. Then give me wisdom—through prayer, through honest evaluation of my abilities and interests, and through the counsel of my teachers, professors, and others to make choices and decisions that will further my pursuit of this goal.

Finally, Lord, help me to believe in myself and to persistently pursue my vision until it becomes my reality.

amen

Chapter Nine

Managing Your Finances

9

Managing Your Finances

Debt management is not in conflict with student loans.
But it is important to know how to manage your debt
before you take out the loan.

Managing your finances is not easy. And when you have debts that must be repaid, it becomes even more difficult. Since many college students will have student loans, and perhaps other debts, to repay after graduation, it's important to learn to manage those debts now, and to learn to plan ahead for life after college.

The following humorous story illustrates how difficult debt management can be:

✧ ✧ ✧

In Washington D.C. a meeting took place between the President, the Chairman of the Federal Reserve, the Budget Director, and God. The men figured they would take advantage of God meeting with them, and they would ask Him some questions.

First, the President asked, "God, I want to know when unemployment will be ended in the United States."

God answered, "Sorry to tell you this, but it's not going to be until the year 2010."

The President said, "Not during my term in office."

The Chairman of the Federal Reserve asked, "When will the prime rate be down to 3%?"

God answered, "That's not going to happen until the year 2020."

The Chairman said, "Not during my term."

Then the Chairman of the Federal Budget Department asked, "When will we have a balanced federal budget?"

God answered, "Not during my term."

The Budget Finance Manager of the United States of America has an extremely difficult job. You may look at yourself and say, "Well, if the country can't do it, how can I be expected to manage my finances in an orderly manner?"

I. WE ARE STEWARDS

Regardless of what others do or don't do, we are responsible for our own lives. We are stewards of all that God has given us. He expects us to be faithful managers of what He gives us.

Jesus told the parable of the talents of money to illustrate what God expects of us (Matthew 25:14-30). In this story a man went on a journey and entrusted each servant with a sum of money. Two of the servants were successful in increasing what they had been given, the third did nothing with what he had been given. When the master returned, he put the first two servants in charge of many things, but he took back the money from the third servant who did nothing.

The point of the story is that if you can take care of little things, you can take care of big things.

Therefore, as college students with limited incomes and resources, it's appropriate that you learn to manage the "little" that you have.

II. CREDIT

Credit is a way of life in the United States. We live in the "Go ahead and get it" age, where we don't have to wait until we have enough money to buy something. We can rent to own, or buy it on credit.

Credit is an amoral thing; it is neither moral nor immoral. Credit is a tool, and like any tool it can be used either for good or bad, for benefit or harm. A chain-saw is also an efficient tool. Just try to cut down a tree with an axe, and you will appreciate what a marvelous invention the chain saw is. But a chain-saw, like credit, can be used in an improper manner. A movie about an incident in Texas described how a chain-saw could be used for the wrong reasons.

Credit, used improperly, can ruin people's lives. It can just hack them up and do horrible things. But credit managed and controlled is a good tool.

Credit is something that exists—something that you either use poorly or you use well.

1. Good uses of credit

A good use of credit would be to purchase something that it is impossible to save enough money to pay cash for. No one in this day and age can reasonably expect to save enough money to pay cash for a house. Credit used to finance a house or other major purchase is considered an investment.

Credit can be used to manage your money. If you are in control of your finances and you have good credit ratings, you can get credit cards that have no annual fee. Then if you pay all your bill when it is due, you pay no interest. In such a case, you may choose to purchase a large expense item, leave the cash accruing interest in your checking account and pay for it all when the bill comes at the end of the month. You actually make money with a credit card when you use it in that way.

For some people, however, this can be dangerous. They make the purchase and have good intentions to pay it off at the due date. But in the meantime, they spend the cash which is set aside. Great self-discipline is required to handle credit in this manner.

2. Help for out-of-control spenders

A credit manager had the following suggestion for people who have trouble with credit cards, but would like to keep one card for emergencies.

Pay off all credit cards but one, and get rid of them. Pay off that one credit card and keep it for emergencies. But do not keep it where it is readily accessible. Wrap it in tinfoil, put it in a tin can, fill the can with water, and stick it in the freezer. You have to make a phenomenally conscious decision to use that card. You can't microwave it because it's wrapped in metal. You can't stick it in the oven, because the card might melt. You can't break it open with a hammer because frozen plastic is not durable, and your card might come out in tiny pieces. So you must wait several hours to get access to this credit card.

This may sound extreme, but it is one technique to use when you need help. Other techniques can be used when you can't control credit card spending, but you still need to keep a card for "just in case."

<hr>

Credit used improperly is like a time-bomb ready to explode.

<hr>

Many banks and department stores today will give college students a minimum line of credit. These banks and stores are looking ahead. Their philosophy is that college students will have a higher potential for income earning, so they want to get you started with them while you are in college. That can be dangerous.

One student, in her senior year in college, received several credit cards. Each card had a credit limit. A credit limit doesn't mean that you must charge up to that limit, which this young lady found out to her mistake. She went out and charged those cards to their maximum, then found that even the minimum payment on several cards was more than she could handle.

2. Be wise—calculate the interest

Minimum payment s are much better for the credit card company than for you. If you compute what you pay for items purchased on credit at 19 or 20% interest, which is standard with most credit cards, you will find that you are paying not 20% more than the list price, but 50% to 100% more. A $300 credit bill with minimum $10 payment a month at 19% interest will take a long time to pay off.

III. FINANCIAL AID AND RESOURCES

Many sources of financial aid are available to college students. These sources include:

- ✔ federal government
- ✔ state governments
- ✔ parents and other relatives
- ✔ banks
- ✔ college or school

Information about the various agencies, programs, scholarships, and other resources are listed below. Not all sources are available for all students, but all students should be able to obtain financial aid from some of these sources.

Be aware that programs of this nature change constantly, and the information in this section is based on 1996 sources. Additional, and/or more current material should be available through your college or university.

Pell Grants

These grants are financed by the federal government. They are based on need, and awarded by the school you attend. The Department of Education guarantees that the schools participating in this program receive enough money to pay the Pell Grants of all students who meet eligibility requirements. These grants provide a foundation of financial aid that can be added to from other sources.

Students do not have to repay money received through Pell Grants.

SEOG—Supplemental Educational Opportunity Grants

Unlike the Pell Grant, not every eligible student is able to receive an SEOG. Money available for SEOGs is limited; therefore it is extremely important to apply early.

CWS—College Work-Study

This program is designed to give students an opportunity to earn money to help pay for educational expenses. Hours of work are determined by your class schedules, academic progress, and health. Students receiving Pell Grants are given priority at CWS. The pay scale may vary, but will be at least current minimum wage, and could be more depending on type of work and skills required.

Perkins Loans

These loans are long-term, have low interest rates, and eligibility is based on financial need. Perkins Loans are available from schools that receive money for this purpose. Application deadlines are extremely important since money is limited. After leaving school, the loan is repaid in monthly payments.

Federal Family Education Loan Programs

Specific programs, including Stafford Loans, Supplemental Loans, and the PLUS program, are in this category. These loan programs have traditionally offered low-interest loans from banks, credit unions, or savings and loans. Sometimes the federal government will pay part of the interest on the loan. For current information on these types of loans, check with the financial aid office at your school. Some schools are phasing out these programs and replacing them with direct lending programs funded by the federal government.

Scholarships

Most colleges provide scholarships for outstanding performance in athletics, academics, or the arts. In addition, other smaller scholarships may be available for students pursuing degrees in specific areas. Several fraternal, service, educational, and social organizations like the American Association of University Women, Elks, Rotary, Kiwanis, Sertoma, or Lions often provide grants that don't have to be repaid for local students. Some local school districts, or groups within the districts, also make scholarships available to students who have graduated from their districts.

The Veterans Administration

Money for education is available for some veterans and their dependents. The War Orphans Educational Assistance, Air Force Aid Society, and Army Educational Assistance programs are set up for children of military personnel.

Active Military Personnel

Financial aid programs are available for those in the military. Contact local personnel office for information.

Company Assistance Programs

These programs are set up and funded by employers to assist employees to attend school while they are working.

Social Security Payments

Available for unmarried students, up to age 18, who have a deceased parent or a parent who is disabled or drawing Social Security benefits.

State Vocational Rehabilitation Offices

Students with visual impairments, hearing or speech difficulties, or other physical disabilities can usually obtain financial help through state vocational rehab offices.

The U.S. Bureau of Indian Affairs

Financial aid is available for some Native American students.

Local State Employment Office

Information about two government programs that provide money for going to school is available through your local state employment office. These two programs are: JTPA (Job Training Partnership Act) and WIN (Work Incentive).

Relatives

Don't forget "Aunt Betty" or "Grandpa Jones" as possible resources for financial aid. While family members might not lend you money for a car, a business, or a vacation, many are genuinely pleased to help dedicated students get an education. A straightforward, sincere request will probably be given consideration.

Personal Savings

Is there money available from savings accounts, bonds, stocks, or trusts set up by others to support your education? The bulk of money for higher education comes from these sources.

Employment

Additional money can be obtained through working at a part-time job. And if you can find a job related to your future career field you will benefit educationally as well as financially.

Sell Something

Do you have possessions that you need less than an education? Consider selling it. Maybe, for a little while, you could get along without that car, house, musical instrument, or hobby. You probably won't want to do this except as a last resort, but remember that it is an option. And you want to explore all your options to reach your goal of a college degree.

IV. CAREER

Looking ahead realistically is another facet of debt management. Many college students make the mistake of thinking they can afford to run up a large debt while in school, because they will be making a lot of money when they graduate.

Students may have some information about projected salaries in their profession, but they may fail to consider that they won't be starting out at top dollar. Their entry level salary may even be lower than the median. The Department of Labor, Bureau of U.S. Labor Statistics publishes the *Occupational Outlook Handbook* which gives salary statistics in various jobs. They constantly survey jobs and determine the median salaries as well as the maximum and the minimum. They also give other valuable information about the job market. (Copies are available in the reference section of the library.)

When you consider projected salaries, remember that one-half of all people will fall in the median areas. There's not a lot of difference between the middle 50%. You have the high and low extremes, but almost everybody falls somewhere in that median figure.

So when you start looking at the median salary in your category, the odds are you will be close to the middle figure.

When you consider income distributions, you might have a median of $20,000 with a range of $22,000 high and a low of $18,000. Fifty percent of the people are going to be in this range.

You need to have a realistic idea of what you can expect to make, and take that into consideration as you determine how much credit you can manage.

V. HOW MUCH DO THEY MAKE?

Computer Engineer—Salary $70,000. Opportunities in software for auto, aircraft and equipment safety; also multimedia. Growth is projected to continue through 2005 at a rate of 112%.

Physical therapist—Salary $49,000. Growth projected through 2005 at rate of 88%. Opportunities in pediatrics, neonatal, sports medicine, and in-home health care.

Psychologist; staff/private practice—Salary $33,000/$76,000. Growth through 2005 at rate of 48%. Opportunities in public and private practice in the Southwest.

Registered nurse—Salary $35,620. Growth projected through 2005 at rate of 42%. Opportunities in home nursing and ambulatory care.

Social worker; medical/clinical—Salary $31,500/$38,250. Growth projected through 2005 at 39%. Opportunities in family support and child welfare agencies; team practices.

Teacher; secondary school—Salary $35,880. Growth projected through 2005 at rate of 37%. Opportunities in high-school Spanish, math and the sciences.

Teacher; special education—Salary $33,644. Growth through 2005 at rate of 75%. Opportunities in education for disabled and chronically ill students.

Marketing, advertising, public relations manager—Salary $49,000. Growth through 2005 at rate of 36%. Opportunities in fund-raising and government lobbying firms.

Physician/general surgeon—Salary $156,000/$200,000. Growth through 2005 at rate of 35%. Opportunities in rural hospitals and managed-care facilities.

Accountant and auditor—Salary $37,166. Growth through 2005 at rate of 32%. Opportunities in tax accounting, especially international; estate management.

Lawyer—Salary $58,000. Growth through 2005 at rate of 31%. Opportunities in health care and intellectual property.

Religious director/clergy—Salary $54,350/$27,922. Growth through 2005 at rate of 30%. Opportunities in the Midwest and South; evangelical and media ministries.

> *Regardless of the profession, you will start out in the entry level position, where you will not make top salary. You need to keep that in mind as you're starting to prepare yourself.*

VI. TAXES

When you're projecting how much money you will be able to make, you must also project the amount that you will take home. You must consider that taxes will take big bites out of your big bucks. First, there is the FICA; 7.51% of your salary will be automatically taken out for FICA. Allegedly, you'll see that when you are sixty-five. There are also federal and state income taxes. Taxes will take some of your money. Realistically—if you're single, taxes will take a **lot** of your money.

While you are in college, you do not have to pay much tax, so you need to be prepared for the adjustment you will have to make after graduation. If you work while you're in college, you may not have anything withheld for taxes. Or if you do have something withheld, you get it back every year.

In your senior year of college, you will need to make a change on your exemptions for taxes. If you do not change your student exemption tax status after graduation, you will find that at the end of the year you could owe the Federal Government $500 or $600.

VII. OTHER EXPENSES AFTER GRADUATION

A projected salary of $20,000 or more may look like a lot to you now while you're in college. But in addition to the taxes that will come out of that, you will have other expenses that you do not have as a student.

You will need to buy professional business clothes, because you have to dress better at work than at college. You may have to buy furniture, rent or buy a house, buy a car or a better car.

When you get married, other financial adjustments have to be considered. If you and your spouse both have $20,000 yearly incomes, that will put you in a higher tax bracket than when you were single. And you may owe $500 or $600 to the IRS at the end of the year.

Plan ahead. If you're going to make a change in your life, think about the change in taxes. The IRS will.

VIII. CASH MANAGEMENT

People have been heard to say, "I don't make enough money to live on a budget." But think about it realistically:

If you're bringing home just a little bit of money, you really need a budget. If you don't plan and budget, you'll always have more month than money.

Then if you try to finish the month on credit cards, you start a spiral effect where you charge more on your credit cards each month than you pay on them and they get bigger and bigger. One card gets full, and you start using another one. Your debts just pile up.

Learning to manage your money and live on the money you make is so important. Don't wait until you are sixty-five and retire and think that you can live on your Social Security. Talk to people who are trying to live on Social Security now. They will tell you that it is not enough to live on.

IX. PLAN NOW FOR YOUR FUTURE

You need to plan for your own future. And the only way you're going to plan for the future is to plan for today. Learn to live each month within what you bring home in that month.

Plan for expenses that don't occur every month, like car insurance. Plan wisely and pay for your car insurance in one lump sum payment as opposed to paying their 12% or 15% interest for making payments over a six-month period.

If you set aside one-sixth of your policy each month in your bank account, then at the end of six months, when it's time to renew, you can pay cash. That way you make the payments to yourself and not to the insurance company. You collect the interest and not someone else. It really works.

A newspaper recently carried the phenomenal story of a man who was making a $15,000,000 donation to a school for a scholarship fund. He had worked for UPS all of his life, and retired in the early 1960s as an executive. The most that man ever made in a year was $14,000. Yet he was worth $7,000,000 when he retired because he had invested in company stocks. Over the years, he wisely invested his money and took care of it. By 1990 his net worth was $30,000,000, and he decided to give half of that to a college for a scholarship fund.

All this, and he never made more than $14,000 a year in his life. It's true that $14,000 in 1960 had more buying power than it has today. Still, how many people making $60,000 a year today will have $7,000,000 set aside by the time they retire, and then turn that into $30,000,000 over the next thirty years. That man was a wise steward of his money. He made good use of God's blessings.

1. Plan your expenses realistically

Many people plan their expenses for the month and do not allot anything for entertainment. That isn't realistic for most people—especially college students. Be realistic. Plan what you want to do for entertainment on the average month. If you like to go to movies, go to the $1 theaters instead of the $7 theaters. You can see seven times as many movies.

If you like to go out with friends for pizza, you can take advantage of the advertised specials.

2. Paying off student loans

If you will have student loans to pay off when you graduate, you need to figure that in your budget. You might even add $5 or $10 more each month to your minimum required payment. Not only will you pay it off earlier, but you will also save on interest charges.

There are a lot of little things you can do—things that are practically painless—that will pay big dividends later.

3. Savings

Save something every month—even if it's only a small amount. That savings will help you on the day that you have an emergency, the day you get laid off, or the day your company goes bankrupt.

A good financial planning technique is to keep at least three months' salary in a savings account that is accessible—not invested in the stock market—but in CDs or funds that you can get to if you have an emergency. Be prepared for real life.

4. Resources on cash management

Your university will probably have many available resources on cash management. Books and computer programs can give you information on specific careers. They can forecast either an increasing or decreasing job market in your chosen field. Take advantage of these resources.

Don't let your finances control you. Control your own finances.

Chapter Nine

Discussion Questions and Exercises

1. Use the chart on this page and the next to develop a plan for spending your money month to month. Each month, examine the previous month's budget and use the information to refine your saving and spending plan.

BUDGET ___/___/___

Money In From:	This Month	Next Month
1 _____	_____	_____
2 _____	_____	_____
3 _____	_____	_____
4 _____	_____	_____
5 _____	_____	_____
6 _____	_____	_____
7 _____	_____	_____
8 _____	_____	_____
9 _____	_____	_____
10 _____	_____	_____
Total Cash Income (add 1–10)	$	$

(continue on next page)

Money Out To:	This Month	Next Month
11 _____	_____	_____
12 _____	_____	_____
13 _____	_____	_____
14 _____	_____	_____
15 _____	_____	_____
16 _____	_____	_____
17 _____	_____	_____
18 _____	_____	_____
19 _____	_____	_____
20 _____	_____	_____
21 _____	_____	_____
22 _____	_____	_____
23 _____	_____	_____
24 _____	_____	_____
25 _____	_____	_____
26 _____	_____	_____
27 _____	_____	_____
28 _____	_____	_____

Total Cash Expenses
(add 11-28)

$	$

Money Left
Subtract Total Out from Total In

$	$

2. Describe an aspect of your financial life that is not working as well as you would like right now. List two options for solving your money problem. List 5 specific strategies you could use to increase your income or decrease your expenses.

Problem:

_____

_____

_____

_____

_____

_____

Options:

1. _____

_____

_____

2. _____

_____

_____

_____

Strategies:

1. _____

_____

_____

2. _____

_____

_____

3. _____

_____

_____

4. _____

_____

_____

5. _____

_____

_____

♥ ♥ ♥

Scripture and Prayer

And my God will meet all your needs according to his glorious riches in Christ Jesus. Philippians 4:19 NIV

Heavenly Father,

Thank you for your promise to supply all my needs. Give me the ability to distinguish between a need and a want, and to be willing to postpone some of the wants while I trust you for the needs.

I realize that you probably have many ways to supply the things I need, so help me to recognize and be thankful for your provision whether it comes through a job I work at, through support from parents and family, through scholarships, or other means. Regardless of how the provision comes, or the amount of the provision, help me to manage my finances wisely. Thank you for faculty, counselors, and older students who can help me to set up a budget and make wise decisions about credit and student loans.

Help me, Lord, to be a good steward of all that you have provided.

amen

Chapter Ten

Stress: What Is It,
and How Do I Control It?

Dr. Larry W. Barron

10

Stress: What is it?

Personality traits do affect the way we respond to and cope with stress. But we can all learn to better handle the stress that from time to time will come to all of us.

1. HANS SELYE'S RESEARCH AND THEORY

Hans Selye, one of the great pioneers in the area of stress research, had two definitions for stress. The first was very simple: "The rate of wear and tear within the body." The second was much more abstract: "The state manifested by a specific syndrome which consists of all the non-specifically induced changes within a biologic system" (Selye, 1956). Selye believed that a person under stress goes through a series of processes or stages, termed the General Adaptation Syndrome:

1. Alarm is the first stage. This is where the person becomes aware of the "stressor," and immediately "the body's entire stress mechanism is mobilized" (Pelletier, 1977). Imagine yourself walking down a dark alley at night; suddenly, you hear a growling noise and a huge, black Doberman, fangs bared, lunges at you. You're getting a pretty good idea of what "Alarm" is, aren't you? Your body gets ready for a "Fight-or-Flight" response, where you will either try to defeat the Stressor (i.e., the big, black dog), or you will try to escape the Stressor (e.g., run like mad!). Some of your body's reactions include:

- ✔ a racing, pounding heart
- ✔ a soaring blood pressure
- ✔ a flooding of hormones (including epinephrine or adrenalin, especially during fear; and norepinephrine, especially during rage/anger)
- ✔ a quickening of breathing
- ✔ a tensing of muscles (Tanner, 1976)

2. Resistance is the second stage. During this time, your body is continuing to fight off (cope with) the Stressor, and usually succeeds in doing so.

3. Exhaustion is the last stage. Unfortunately, the costs of fighting stress are many (we will discuss some of these later), and a person's body may start "wearing out" in one or more ways. If this occurs, the person has now reached the Exhaustion Stage, and may start to manifest one or more psychophysiological reactions to stress.

While this portrayal of stress paints a grim picture, Selye insisted that some forms of stress are actually beneficial. Thus, he differentiated "good stress" (eustress) from "bad stress" (distress).

II. SOCIAL READJUSTMENT RATING SCALE

Many psychologists agree with Selye's assessment. For example, Holmes and Rahe feel that stress is a result of change—regardless of whether the change is positive or negative. Thus, positive events in our lives that require change (marriage, retirement, vacations) may be as stressful as negative, life-changing events (divorce, personal injury, jail term). To show this, Holmes and Rahe (1967) devised a 100-point scale, and arbitrarily chose "Marriage" as being worth 50 stress points. They then asked respondents to rank order and classify stressful events from 0 to 100, using Marriage as the grounding point. As you can see from Table 1 (on the following page), which contains the Social Readjustment Rating Scale (SRRS), very few events are more stressful than getting married—it comes in seventh on their scale. Only six events are more stressful:

As you will see from the chart, stress is closely associated with loss: loss of relationships, loss of freedom, loss of health, loss of status.

Stress is also closely associated with a loss of control; for example, social psychological studies on crowding show that being crowded is stressful, but is a much less negative event if its duration is predictable and reasonably short (Tanner, 1976).

172

Table 1	The social readjustment rating scale		
Life event	Value	Life event	Value
Death of spouse	100	Outstanding personal achievement	28
Divorce	73	Wife begins or stops work	26
Marital separation	65	Begin or end school	26
Jail term	63	Change in living conditions	25
Death of close family member	63	Revision of personal habits	24
Personal injury or illness	53	Trouble with boss	23
Marriage	50	Change in work hours or conditions	20
Fired at work	47	Change in residence	20
Marital reconciliation	45	Change in schools	20
Retirement	45	Change in recreation	19
Change in health of family member	44	Change in church activities	19
Pregnancy	40	Change in social activites	18
Sex difficulties	39	Mortgage or loan less than $10,000	17
Gain of new family member	39	Change in sleeping habits	16
Business readjustment	39	Change in number of family get-togethers	15
Change in financial state	38	Change in eating habits	15
Death of a close friend	37	Vacation	13
Change to different line of work	36	Christmas	12
Change in number of arguments with spouse	35	Minor violations of the law	11
Mortgage over $10,000	31		
Foreclosure of mortgage or loan	30		
Change in responsibilities at work	29		
Son or daughter leaving home	29		
Trouble with in-laws	29		

Source: Adapted from Holmes, T.H., & Rahe, R.H. The Social Readjustment Rating Scale. Journal of Psychosomatic Research, *1967,* 11, *213-218.*

Holmes and Rahe found that eighty percent of the people with an SRRS score exceeding 300 in one year became depressed, had heart attacks, or developed other serious illnesses. I mentioned in the prologue what a stressful time I had back in 1980. You can now see even more clearly why this was true:

65	a breakup
37	a friend's death
36	a new job
28	a personal achievement— (my dissertation)
26	graduation
24	a revision of habits (for me it was getting used to a rural environment and cold winters)
20	change in residence
20	change in schools
15	change in number of family get-togethers
15	change in eating habits
13	vacation
12	Christmas

My grand total was 311. No wonder I was feeling down!

There have been some criticisms of Holmes and Rahe's scale, however. Four of these will be discussed briefly. The first is that not everyone will feel the effects of stress in the same way—individual differences must be considered. (An amusing illustration of this point occurred a few years ago in one of my classes. I was discussing research that stated that married people live about a year longer than divorced persons, and one recent divorcee spoke up and said,

"Well, it was worth a year to get rid of him!" Somehow, I don't feel she should receive 73 stress points for her divorce!)

A second point is that coping differences must also be considered. Some people have a wide array of coping skills that they utilize; others have far fewer and will thus be susceptible more quickly to Selye's Exhaustion state (Hinkle, in Tanner, 1976). Some people could theoretically withstand a build-up of 300 (or more) points, while others would suffer burnout or other stress-related symptoms with much lower scale scores. (Coping skills will be considered at the end of this chapter).

A third problem is that some critics feel that too much emphasis is placed on change; it should be mentioned that lack of change may also be stressful (e.g., being stuck in a dead-end job).

Finally, some critics feel that the SRRS puts too much emphasis on the "big" events in one's life, and ignores the "daily hassles" (e.g., crying babies, barking dogs) that one may encounter (Kanner et al., in Santrock, 1990).

III. PERSONALITY DIFFERENCES

There is a growing body of research that is finding a link between stress and our psychophysiological well-being. In other words, stress is affecting us physiologically, as well as psychologically. Such diseases as cardiovascular heart disease (CHD), peptic ulcers diabetes, colitis, asthma and hypertension are just a few of the disorders researchers are now linking with stress (Insel & Moos, 1974; Tanner, 1976; Pelletier, 1977; Santrock 1990).

How does stress affect us in these ways? The answer seems to be a function of how we perceive the threat (for example, some people perceive stressful events as a challenge, whereas others see them as terrifying), as well as our lifestyle. Thus, personality factors seem to play a mediating role. For example, classic research by Friedman and Rosenman (1974) has divided people into two categories: Type A and Type B. Type A individuals, according to Logan Wright, are characterized by four traits:

✔ A sense of time urgency (e.g., a constant irritation with long lines or slow traffic).

✔ Chronic activation (e.g., they are active all day, every day).

✔ Multiphasia (e.g., they like to do two things at once, such as reading a book while watching television).

✔ Anger\hostility (Fisher, 1987).

In contrast, Type B individuals are typically less worried about time, have a lower activation level, do one thing at a time, and are not as angry\hostile.

Which group do you think is more "at-risk" for stress-related symptoms? If you said Type A, you are right! Wright believes that only two of the elements (hostility and time urgency) are related to stress-related illnesses (especially CHD) (Fisher, 1987), while other psychologists believe the whole cluster

of symptoms is problematic (Fischman, in Santrock, 1990). There is also research that indicates that even suppressed anger may be hard on the heart (Angier, 1990).

The implications, whomever you believe, are clear: personality traits do affect the way we respond to and cope with stressors. Changing one's personality to be less hostile and less anxious (about time, relationships, grades, etc.) seems to be a good first step.

To see if you are a Type A person, I invite you to take Dr. Archibald Hart's Type-A Behavior Pattern Test (see Table 2 on the following page). If you scored in the 0 to 5 range, you are not a Type A; if you scored 6 to 10, you are an occasional Type A; if you scored 11 to 16, you are a Type A; and if you scored 17 to 24, you are not only a Type A, but you are living dangerously (Hart, 1986).

We have discussed how stress affects us in various ways. To learn more about the effects of stress on your body, please take Dr. Hart's second stress test, entitled Symptoms of Distress (see Table 3 —follows table 2). It is scored somewhat similarly to the other test: 0 to 10 (no stress); 11 to 20 (mild stress); 21 to 30 (moderate stress); 31 to 40 (severe stress); and 41 to 60 (dangerous stress).

You may have discovered, to your chagrin, that you are a Type A and that you are experiencing stressful symptoms. The good news is that you can cope! Let's now discuss several methods by which you can deal effectively with stress.

V. STRESS MANAGEMENT:
Acquiring and Using Coping Skills

Lazarus and Folkman (1984) have examined the various methods of coping, and have placed them into two categories: emotion-focused and problem-focused coping. Emotion-focused coping strategies, as the name implies, are more irrational ways of dealing with conflicts, and include denial and withdrawal, among others. Denial involves acting as if the stress does not exist (Santrock, 1990). Current research shows that denial may be a good strategy in the short run, under some occasions, especially if the person can do nothing to change his/her circumstances (Burger, 1990).

For example, research on the psychology of death and dying has shown that denial is indeed one of the more common first reactions to a patient's learning of his own impending death. It is also a common reaction among the survivors, as well, and seems to play an important role in minimizing shock (Kubler-Ross, 1969). There is also research showing that withdrawal, under some circumstances, may be effective (e.g., some children handle their parents' divorce by simply withdrawing and removing themselves from the conflict).

Table 2   Type-A Behavior Pattern Test

Read each question carefully and give yourself a rating according to the following descriptions:

Rating	Description
0	This statement does not apply to me.
1	It sometimes (less than once a month) applies to me.
2	It often (more than once a month) applies to me.

_____ 1.   I feel as if there isn't enough time in each day to do all the things I need to do.

_____ 2.   I tend to speak faster than other people, even finishing their sentences for them.

_____ 3.   My spouse or friends say, or I believe, that I eat too quickly.

_____ 4.   I tend to get very upset whenever I lose a game.

_____ 5.   I am very competitive in work, sports, or games.

_____ 6.   I tend to be bossy and dominate others.

_____ 7.   I prefer to lead rather than follow.

_____ 8.   I feel pressed for time even when I am not doing something important.

_____ 9.   I become impatient when I have to wait.

_____ 10. I tend to make decisions quickly, even impulsively.

_____ 11. I regularly take on more than I can accomplish.

_____ 12. I become irritable (even angry) more often than most other people.

_____   TOTAL

Table 3   Symptoms of Distress

Answer the questions listed below according to the following scale:

Rating	Description
0	I do not experience this symptom at all.
1	I sometimes (perhaps once a month) experience this symptom.
2	I experience this symptom more than once a month, but not more than once a week.
3	I experience this symptom often (more than once a week).

_____1.   Do you experience headaches of any sort?

_____2.   Do you experience tension or stiffness in your neck, shoulders, jaw, arms, hands, legs, or stomach?

_____3.   Do you have nervous tics, or do you tremble?

_____4.   Do you feel your heart thumping or racing?

_____5.   Do you get irregular heartbeats, or does your heart skip beats?

_____6.   Do you have difficulty breathing at times?

_____7.   Do you ever get dizzy or lightheaded?

_____8.   Do you feel as though you have a lump in your throat or you have to clear it?

_____9.   Do you suffer from colds, the flu, or hoarseness?

_____10.   Are you bothered by indigestion, nausea, or discomfort in your stomach?

_____11.   Do you have diarrhea or constipation?

_____12.   Do you bite your nails?

_____13.   Do you have difficulty falling or staying asleep?

_____14.   Do you wake up feeling tired?

_____15.   Are your hands or feet cold?

_____16.   Do you grind or grit your teeth, or do your jaws ache?

_____17.   Are you prone to excess perspiration?

_____18.   Are you angry or irritable?

_____19.   Do you feel a lot of generalized pain (back pain, stomach pain, head pain, muscle pain, etc.)?

_____20.   Have you become aware of increased anxiety, worry, fidgetiness or restlessness?

_____   **TOTAL**

The more recommended strategies are the problem-focused methods. In these strategies, the person tackles the problem head-on and tries to solve it. One must ask himself/herself, "What is the problem here? What is it that I want? What steps can I take? What will be the outcome of these steps? Shall I do it?" (Finally, assuming the action is taken), "How did it turn out?" (Phares, 1988).

Two good examples of problem-solving techniques from Morris (1990) include:

✔ Sub-goaling (breaking the problem into sections and solving each part successively).

✔ Working backwards (starting at the endpoint and working back towards the beginning point).

For example, suppose you are faced with constructing a major term paper for one of your classes. You could deny that it exists (and many students do, right up until the night before it is due!), but that is not an effective strategy (you're trying to minimize stress, remember!).

You could also withdraw by going to a movie or concert, but that will not get the job done either. So, start with Sub-goaling: break the "monster" into steps: selecting a topic, gathering research (from the school's library as well as from inter-library loan), planning the paper, writing it (in sections), proofreading, reorganizing, and finally typing it. Also work backwards from the day it's due: how much time do you need

for typing, proofreading, writing, gathering research, etc.? By working backwards, you should get a good idea of when you need to begin working on the paper.

Other excellent stress-management ideas come from Phares (1988):

1. Reduce tension (by passively riding out the event, ignoring the situation for awhile, letting the tension wear off, or engaging in unrelated activities—such as exercise or hobbies, just carrying on as usual, getting out of the situation temporarily and seeking advice from others, seeing the humor in the situation, and doing relaxation exercises).

2. Use cognitive reappraisal: convince yourself that the stressor is not as threatening as you believed—that the stressor is a challenge, not a threat. Bandura (1977) has conducted several studies on the topic of self-efficacy (which means creating an "I-can-do-it" attitude). Research has shown the value of self-efficacy in areas such as losing weight or eliminating bad habits such as smoking (Sears, Peplau & Taylor, 1991). It is felt that an "I-can-do-it" attitude may be used to reduce the threats in one's life.

3. Find and utilize your own social support network: talk over problems with others, whether they be friends, parents, teachers, pastors, counselors, etc. (Phares, 1988).

Other excellent tips include:

- ✔ Evaluating each situation realistically (rather than being the ever-enthusiastic optimist or the perpetual doom-sayer).
- ✔ Being honest with yourself by shunning the "super-hero" urge (recognizing your limits).
- ✔ Taking one thing at a time.
- ✔ Balancing work and relaxation.
- ✔ Eating a balanced diet.
- ✔ Getting enough rest and sleep.
- ✔ Channeling your anger by doing something constructive (e.g., through a physical workout).
- ✔ Giving in once in a while.
- ✔ Making yourself available to others (without being too pushy!).
- ✔ Doing something for others.
- ✔ Learning to accept what you cannot change.

- ✔ Praying can be one of your most beneficial means to relieve stress, especially when prayer is a regular part of your life. (Although some "foxhole Christians" pray only when they are in trouble, "it's curious how many otherwise dedicated Christians fail to pray when they need it most—during times of stress") (*Stress: The Buzz Word of the 1980s,* 1987).

Obviously, not all of these methods are going to work for every situation. You need to experiment for yourself to see which methods are best for you—some will work better under some conditions than others, and still others may not work for you at all. The important reminders are to keep trying, and to be adaptable and flexible. Stress CAN be reduced!

Suggested Activities

1. One former counselor at Western Evangelical Seminary in Portland, Oregon gave this advice: Lie down and concentrate on wiggling your toes for five minute each day. Since you can't concentrate on anything else, your mind will relax.

2. Take "minute" vacations (e.g., daydream for one minute about a favorite place you've been to, or would like to go to) (Hansel, 1979).

3. Monitor your stress level—check yourself periodically (especially heart rate, blood pressure, skin temperature and muscle tension) Braley, 1990).

4. Deliberately slow down (e.g., read a book for enjoyment, not for learning); choose something relaxing; and don't feel guilty about relaxing (Braley, 1990).

5. Resolve emotions that need adrenalin, such as anger (e.g., work on your forgiving attitudes) (Braley, 1990).

6. Review (or create, and then review) your life goals: Which are necessary? What time frame have you used for reaching them? Are the goals and time frames realistic? (Braley, 1990).

7. Relax expectations and enjoy nature (Braley, 1990)—in other words, trite as it may be, take time to stop and smell the roses!

8. Rest! Learn the secret of sleep (i.e., learn how much sleep you really need—it could be as much as ten hours a night) (Braley, 1990).

Suggested Readings

In addition to the books listed in the References Section, any good Introductory Psychology text or Personality Psychology text should give the reader more information on stress and stress management.

References

Angier, N. (1990, December 13). Studies show chronic anger is strong health risk. *The Phoenix Gazette*, p. E1.

Bandura, A. (1977). Self-efficacy: Toward a unifying theory of behavioral change. *Psychological Review, 84,* 191-215.

Braley, J. (1990). Stress: The quiet enemy. Paper presented at the meeting of the Association of Christian Schools International, Phoenix, AZ.

Burger, J. M. (1990) *Personality* (2nd ed.). Belmont, CA: Wadsworth Publishing Company.

Fisher, K. (1987, October). Logan Wright on Type A ingredients. *APA Monitor*, p.8.

Friedman, M., Rosenman, R.H. (1974). *Type A behavior and your heart*. New York; Alfred A. Knoph.

Hart, A.D. (1986). *Adrenalin and stress*. Waco, TX: Word Books.

Hansel, T. (1979). *When I relax I feel guilty*. Weston, ON, Canada: David C. Cook Publishing Company.

Holmes, T., & Rahe, R. H. (1967). The social readjustment rating scale. *Journal of Psychosomatic Research,* 11, 213-218.

Insel, P.M., & Moos, R. H. (Eds.). (1974). *Health and the social environment.* Lexington, MA: D.C. Heath and Company.

Kubler-Ross, E. (1969). *On death and dying*. New York: Macmillan.

Lazarus, R., & Folkman, S. (1984). *Stress, appraisal, and coping*. New York: Springer

Morris, C.G. (1990). *Psychology: An introduction* (7th ed.). Englewood Cliffs, NJ: Prentice Hall.

Pelletier, K.R. (1977) *Mind as healer, mind as slayer*. New York: Delta Books.

Phares, E.J. (1988). *Introduction to personality* (2nd ed.). Glenview, IL: Scott, Foresman and Co.

Santrock, J. W. (199). *Adolescence* (4th ed.). Dubuque, IA: William C. Brown Publishers.

Sears, D. O., Peplau, L. A., & Taylor, S. E. (1991). *Social psychology* (7th ed.). Englewood Cliffs, NJ: Prentice Hall.

Selye, H. (1956) *The stress of life*. New York:

McGraw-Hill. Stress: The buzz word of the '80s. (1987, July). *SBC Benefits Bulletin,* pp. 2-3.

Tanner, O. (1976). *Stress*. New York: Time-Life Books.

Chapter Ten

Discussion Questions and Exercises

Checklist for Sources of Stress

The following situations commonly cause mental and physical stress. Check the items that you have experienced in the past year.

School

- ☐ Entered college for the first time
- ☐ Transferred to a new school
- ☐ Too many courses
- ☐ Too much homework
- ☐ Serious problem with professor
- ☐ Failed a course
- ☐ Lower grade than expected
- ☐ Too many classes
- ☐ Worried about grades
- ☐ Dropped more than one course
- ☐ On academic probation

Family

- ☐ Close relative died
- ☐ Close relative seriously ill or injured
- ☐ Serious problem with relative
- ☐ Moved and left close relatives
- ☐ Separated or divorced
- ☐ Parent lost job

Friends

- ☐ Close friend died
- ☐ Close friend seriously ill or injured
- ☐ Serious problem with close friend
- ☐ Moved and left close friends
- ☐ Not enough friends

Love and Marriage

- ☐ New love interest
- ☐ Became engaged or married
- ☐ Became pregnant
- ☐ Became a parent
- ☐ Sexual problems
- ☐ Serious problem with partner
- ☐ Trouble with in-laws
- ☐ Divorced or separated
- ☐ Couldn't find desired partner
- ☐ Felt physically unattractive

Work

- ☐ Unemployed
- ☐ Dislike job
- ☐ Serious problem with boss or co-worker
- ☐ Fired or laid off
- ☐ Worried about losing job
- ☐ Started new job

Money

- ☐ Not enough money for school
- ☐ Not enough money for food, clothing, or housing
- ☐ Not enough money for car or entertainment
- ☐ Worried about debts
- ☐ Failed to get credit card or loan
- ☐ Took out large loan

Living Place

- ☐ Not enough space or privacy
- ☐ Annoying neighbor
- ☐ Bad neighborhood
- ☐ Moved to a new place
- ☐ Denied living in a desired place
- ☐ Problem with roommate
- ☐ Too many responsibilities

Health

- ☐ Seriously ill or injured
- ☐ Unable to get needed medical or dental care
- ☐ Abused alcohol or drugs

♥ ♥ ♥

Scripture and Prayer

*God is our refuge and strength, an ever-present help in trouble. Therefore we will not fear....*Psalm 46:1-2, NIV
O my people, listen! For I am your God....I want you to trust me in your times of trouble, so I can rescue you, and you can give me glory. Psalm 50:7 & 15, TLB
...in quietness and confidence is your strength....
Isaiah 30:15, TLB

Heavenly Father,

I realize that this time in college will often be stressful. So, right now, in the beginning of my college career, I need your help in learning positive techniques to deal with stress and to avoid the build-up of stress. Thank you for the information in this chapter. Help me to remember it and refer back to it in stressful times.

Lord, help me to daily practice the good habits and routines that contribute to a reduction in levels of stress. Help me to be realistic and honest concerning my physical, mental, and emotional limits. Help me to make wise decisions—such as getting enough rest, eating a balanced diet, taking time to relax, etc., for I know that a healthful, balanced lifestyle will help me to deal with the stress I cannot avoid rather than adding to it.

But most of all, Lord, help me to trust you, knowing that you are Lord of all, and that you have everything in control whether I can see it or feel it. By faith, I can choose to believe your word and come again to that place of quiet confidence which is the source of great strength.

amen

Keeping Faith

Fill My Cup, Lord

Leslie Dodrill, PH.D.

11

Keeping Faith

We are not the source of love—we are the channels! We accept God's love into our lives, and then we overflow into the lives of others.

Entering college is a time of great change. No doubt you have many questions waiting to be answered. Some of these questions may be in regard to your faith. Perhaps the secret cry of your heart might even be something like this:

"Lord, I'm so lonesome. I left all my family and friends behind. In this transient society, nothing is constant. I can't depend upon anyone to always be there when I need them! "

"Lord, are you real?"

"Lord, you know I attend church every Sunday, but somehow I feel empty, depressed. There's got to be more. I believe with all my heart you are the answer—but how do I find it?"

"Lord...." Have you ever come to your Lord with any of these questions? Good. I have, too. In fact, I've prayed all of them at one time or another. And because you are willing to admit you have questions, this chapter was written, prayerfully, for you. For I truly believe with all my heart that if you come seeking, asking Him to fill your cup, He will quench the thirsting of your soul. Get your cup ready. Come anticipating. God is going to answer.

First, I would like to share with you some answers that God has shared with me. One of the most important lessons I have ever learned is found in John 21:15-17:

> *"So when they had eaten breakfast, Jesus said to Simon Peter, 'Simon, son of Jonah, do you love me more than these?' He said to Him, 'Yes, Lord; You know that I love You.' He said to Him, 'Feed My lambs.'*
>
> *He said to him again a second time, 'Simon, son of Jonah, do you love me?' He said to Him, 'Yes Lord; You know that I love You.' He said to him, 'Tend My sheep.'*
>
> *He said to him the third time, 'Simon, son of Jonah, do you love Me?' Peter was grieved because He said to him the third time, 'Do you love Me?' And he said to Him, 'Lord, You know all things; You know that I love You.' Jesus said to him, 'Feed My sheep.'"*

This is a familiar story and many great sermons have been preached from it. I would like to suggest a possible interpretation.

Notice that Jesus asked Peter three times, *"Do you love me?"* Why three times? Perhaps each time Jesus asked, He spoke with emphasis on a different word, giving each question a different nuance of meaning. The first time Jesus asked, perhaps He emphasized the word *you. "Do you, Peter, love me?"* I can imagine the eyes of Jesus focused directly upon Peter. Eyes full of compassion, but eyes penetrating the face of the fallen disciple. *"Do you, **Peter,** not the other eleven, not your brother, not your family, but do you, Peter, love me?"*

Peter could not avert his eyes from that remarkable gaze. He looked directly into the face of Christ.

The full impact of that startles me. Jesus is looking directly at me. He is asking, "Leslie, do *you* love me?" He is not asking about my husband, my grandmother, my friends, my pastor — He is asking me. I can avoid neither His face nor His question.

Perhaps the second time Jesus asked the question, He emphasized the word love. "Peter do you *love* me?" What is love? "I love my husband," "I love my dog," "I love spinach." Ambiguous, huh? But here Jesus is talking about the highest form of love—not a casual acquaintance, but a deep abiding personal commitment. Love as action. Love putting into practice the words I say with my lips.

And perhaps the final time Jesus spoke to Peter, He asked, *"Peter, do you love Me?"* Not the church, not the pastor, not the music director, but Me, Jesus Christ. Not the special music that makes you gasp with awe, not the eloquent prayer that lifts you heavenward, not all your Christian friends in your Sunday School class, not even what Christ did for you by giving His life on the cross for your sins. . . but Me, Jesus Christ.

We relish the affection of our families when they tell us that they love us for making good grades, winning a scholarship, hitting a home run. . . but what we really want to hear them say is, "I love you — for you — for just being you." Jesus wants us to love him for just being Jesus—and to tell Him so, sometimes.

Now, the Big Question: How can I love Christ more?

Ask yourself, "How do I fall in love with someone?" You'll probably reply, "First, I have to get to know that person." How do I do that? I spend time with the person. Here is our answer: Spending time with Jesus. Falling more and more in love with Christ. That is the essence of the Christian walk, the heart of Christian growth.

How do I begin? By spending time with Christ. Some people do this through quiet time, some through prayer and Bible reading; I prefer *Practicing the Presence of God.* It is God and me being alone together, getting to know each other. The following guidelines may help you "Practice His Presence:"

I. Give God the Best Part of Your Day

Now, everything I have read says to have quiet time early in the morning, and there are many scriptures to indicate this to be the best time. However, I am not a morning person. My body may be up and moving, but I am never awake before 9:30! Some students don't come alive until midnight! Know your own personality. Pick a time that is right for you, when you are at your **very best**, and dedicate those moments to God every day.

II. Desire Quality More Than Quantity

Pick a book of the Bible, chapter 1, verse 1, and begin reading. You can either read a pre-determined amount—so many chapters or pages, or you might simply read until something catches your attention and you sense that it would be good to stop at that point and ponder what you've read. Either way, take time to think about what you've read. Meditate upon it. Write it down in a notebook or in your Bible. Talk to God about what He wants you to do about what you've learned. Make plans to carry it through. You may read five verses, you may read five chapters. It makes no difference. Remember, this is your chance to be alone with the One who formed your very soul. Listen to what He wants to say to **you**, not your girlfriend or your roommate.

If you are not certain where to start, may I suggest the Book of Philippians, and use a modern translation that you can understand.

III. Do Not Be Discouraged

I have tried daily Bible readings many times in my life. I got all excited about "Read the Bible through in '72." Although I always started with gusto, I would eventually miss a day, then two, then three, then a week, and I would throw up my arms in distress and belittle myself because I was a "no-good, rotten Christian." My thoughts flooded with: "Every good Christian reads his Bible every day. Everyone else can be disciplined. I'm a failure. I can't do it every day, so I must not be able to do it at all." Have you been there?

Then someone helped me to see that having a daily quiet time is a little like eating. There are days when, because of my hectic schedule, I actually miss a meal. Do I throw up my hands in disgust and moan that I am not a good eater because I cannot discipline myself to eat three meals a day? Do I count myself a failure, and decide that I am going to give up eating for the rest of my life! No, of course not. What do I do? I eat twice as much the next time!

Do the same thing spiritually. If you miss a day, try to spend twice as much time the next day. Tell the Father you are sorry for missing your "date" the day before, ask His forgiveness, and then sit at His feet and enjoy the sweet fellowship.

Do not rob yourself of the joy of being with Jesus by accepting the lie that, if you cannot discipline yourself to do devotions daily, you cannot do them at all. I guarantee that you will miss a few days, but pick right back up and continue falling in love with Jesus.

BEGIN NOW! If you have never tried before, there's no time like today. If you already have a daily quiet time, perhaps you need to double-check your attitude. Perhaps you have been doing it just because Christians are supposed to, or to gain "brownie points" with God, and the whole idea of devotions has become a drudgery. Just think, **this is your opportunity to be with God,** to know Him better, to fall in love with Him more.

IV. Use What God Gives You

Matthew 7:6 says: *"Do not give what is holy to the dogs; nor cast your pearls before swine, lest they trample them under their feet...."*

What are these "pearls?" They are beautiful truths which God has shared with us, His children. In this context, the term probably refers to a non-believing world that cannot understand the teachings of God. But it also applies to Christians. The Big Question is:

✔ Why should God give me new pearls if I am not using the ones He has already given me?

✔ Why should God try to teach me Lesson Number Two when I have forgotten Lesson Number One?

✔ Why should God try to teach me Lesson Number Five, when I am ignoring Lesson Number Four?

Many times we keep God from working in our lives because we purposely refuse to obey what He has already taught us. For instance, if you have read the scripture, and understand that God tells his people to tithe, and yet you refuse to do so—for whatever reason—how can God teach you any truths? You are trampling on a pearl He has already tried to give you.

There was a time in my life when a family member had done something that hurt me very badly. I never said anything to her, but I was harboring a grudge and bad thoughts. I tried to read my Bible and to find solace in being with God. But I could not talk to God, for I knew He would tell me to forgive, and I didn't want to do that. So I ignored God's teachings—and ignored God as well. After about a week, God whispered, "Leslie, why don't you forgive her? You are so miserable. Love her as she is, and then you and I can talk." I retaliated: "I like being miserable, God! Leave me alone. She started it and I will not forgive her!"

Another week passed. Finally, when my loneliness could stand it no more, I said, "Father, I forgive her. Father, I ask your forgiveness for not forgiving her earlier, and I ask that our fellowship be restored." A miracle happened. I felt alive and well again! God was my Friend, and we were once again sharing together. I thought to myself, "How stupid! If I had forgiven that person on Day One, I would not have had to spend three miserable weeks." I was self-destructing by deliberately ignoring the Bible truth God had taught me long before.

But more frequently, we waste the pearls God has already given us. For many years, I wasted some of my precious pearls. I forgot the good sermons I heard; I lost the fruit of my Bible studies. I would have a moment of inspiration, of new excitement, and then forget what I had heard. It was not that I wasn't dedicated—I simply didn't retain. So I began writing down what God was teaching me.

I tried several methods: I wrote on the Sunday bulletin, or on other scraps of paper, but eventually these were all thrown out. I tried using a notebook, but I did not always have it handy when I needed it. So now I write in my Bible. If a passage has meaning in my quiet time, I underline or note the meaning. Sometimes, I date it. From the sermon or Sunday School lesson, I translate or describe key words, jot down key ideas, even sometimes outline the entire sermon.

You ask, Where can we gather pearls? I have never heard a sermon or Bible study lesson from God's Word in which I could not discover a pearl to take home with me, **IF** I was searching for it. Sometimes I have been preoccupied about classes, or about some financial problem, or about a sore toe, and never learned a thing. But for these I blame myself, not God or the preacher or the teacher. I've heard the best, and I've heard the worst, and I've always found a pearl when I went looking for one.

V. Keep your cup full

You cannot give away what you do not have! Notice the order in the conversation between Jesus and Simon Peter: "Love me," then "Feed my sheep." Typically, we get this all wrong, especially those of us in leadership roles in our churches and on our campuses.

Our lives are like a bathtub with the drain plug always open. We open the faucet to full strength and squirt a little bath soap in, and soon we have a bathtub overflowing with bubbles. What happens when we turn off the faucet? The water rapidly begins to go down the drain hole, and all that is left is the residue.

We are not the source of love— we are the channel! We accept God's love into our lives, and then we overflow into the lives of others.

When you catch yourself being sharp and critical with others, it's probably because you're not receiving a fresh daily supply of God's love; all that is left in your heart-tub is the residue at the bottom. As we fall in love with Jesus more, we discover a desire to love and feed His sheep.

✔ Fill your heart-tub today.

✔ Overflow into the lives of others.

✔ You cannot give away what you do not have.

I've shared with you in this chapter several pearls in my life. God has used His people, His Word, His Holy Presence to give me these pearls. And, in each case, I have had a choice: to keep them or to lose them.

So, how do I put all these lessons together? By daily seeking God in a personal, intimate way. The Christian life is not finding Jesus as Savior, then graduating on to something higher—or deeper. The Christian life starts with Christ, walks with Christ, and ends with

Christ. Jesus is all of it. The Christian life is knowing Jesus Christ—and knowing Him better.

I'd like to summarize with this illustration. Suppose my sister came to see me on her way to visit our grandmother. "Leslie, come go with me," she begs.

"No, not this time. But you talk to Granny and let me know what she has to say." As she returns, my sister says, "Grandma said to tell you she loves you." I rejoice and I feel good. A week later, she brings the message again, "Grandma says to tell you she loves you." Again and again my sister returns from seeing my grandmother, each time assuring me of her love, "Grandmother said to be sure and tell you she loves you." I never doubt that my sister is telling the truth. I am content to hear the message. After all, I am busy doing good things: I'm feeding the poor, I'm studying for a Bible class, I'm helping a friend. But then, one day, I stop what I'm doing and I go home. I walk up the steps and I peek in the glass door. My grandmother sees me and scurries to greet me. Her face lights up. She opens her arms wide, and she squeezes me tight. She looks into my face: "Leslie, I love you." My heart jumps for joy, My cup runs over.

I have just experienced the most beautiful relationship in the world.

Christians have been going to church for years, hearing secondhand from the preachers, "Jesus said to tell you He loves you." The Sunday School teachers give the message, "He loves you." We accept this truth; we are happy.

But we have robbed ourselves of the joy of hearing the Master say, as He looks personally into our faces, "My child, I LOVE YOU."

Do not rob yourself of the greatest love relationship you can personally experience. Come to the Master with heart held open. Ask Him to fill your cup. He will.

Chapter Eleven

Discussion Questions and Exercises

I. The Presence of Jesus

Spend this next week being in the Presence of Jesus. First, answer the following questions. Next, on the weekly chart, write down the "pearls" you discover in God's Word. Finally, sometime during the week, share at least one pearl with someone else—a roommate, parent, or friend.

1. Do I love God? _____

   _____

2. Do I know God? _____

   _____

3. Do I spend time with God? _____

   _____

4. Do I want to know him better? _____

   _____

5. Have I lost any of the pearls God has tried to give me? Am I doing anything to keep them—day by day, year by year? _____

   _____

   _____

6. Am I living out of the drain hole of my life, or out of the overflow of God's love? _____

   _____

   _____

I Have Come to PRACTICE THE PRESENCE OF GOD!

Sunday: _____

_____

_____

Monday: _____

_____

_____

Tuesday: _____

_____

_____

Wednesday: _____

_____

_____

Thursday: _____

_____

_____

Friday: _____

_____

_____

Saturday: _____

_____

_____

Bible Studies

Because Bible study is foundational to "Keeping Faith," the following exercises are designed to help you establish a fruitful and systematic study of God's Word. Each exercise focuses on a particular topic. Look up and write out each scripture reference in your preferred translation of the Bible. Then answer the questions on each.

Love

1. Matthew 22:37-38 _____

    _____

    _____

    _____

    _____

    a. Who spoke these words? _____
    b. We are to love God with _____

    _____

2. John 13:34-35 _____

    _____

    _____

    _____

How are we to love others? _____

People will know we are Christ's disciples by our _____

3. 1 Corinthians 13:4-7 _____

    _____

    _____

    _____

    _____

    _____

a. Three attributes of love are: _____

_____

b. Love rejoices in the _____

4. 1 Corinthians 13:13 _____

_____

_____

_____

a. Which is greater—faith, hope, or love? _____

Faith

It would be good to read the entire chapter of Hebrews 11.

1. Hebrews 11:1 & 2 _____

_____

_____

_____

_____

a. Faith is _____

_____

2. Hebrews 11:7 _____

_____

_____

_____

a. What did faith cause Noah to do? _____

_____

_____

3. Hebrews 11:10 _____

_____

_____

 a. Through faith, Sarah was able to _____

_____

4. Hebrews 11:23 _____

_____

_____

 a. By faith Moses' parents did what? _____

_____

5. Hebrews 11:30_____

_____

_____

 a. By faith, what fell down? _____

Gifts of God

1. Matthew 6:26 & 33 _____

_____

_____

_____

_____

_____

_____

 a. What are we to seek first? _____
 b. What does God promise to give us? _____

2. 1 Timothy 6:17 _____

_____

_____

_____

   a. God richly provides us with _____

   b. He does this for our _____

3. John 3:16 _____

_____

_____

_____

   a. What did God give the world? _____

   b. What does God give us when we believe in Jesus? _____

4. James 1:5-6 _____

_____

_____

_____

_____

_____

   a. What gift is promised in these verses? _____

   b. What is the requirement to receive this gift? _____

Suggestions for continuing this study

Choose your own topics, using a concordance, such as "Strong's." You could stay with a theme for a week or a month, doing one or two verses per day. Tailor it to your schedule, but make time—take time—for God's Word.

♥ ♥ ♥

Scripture and Prayer

What is faith? It is the confident assurance that something we want is going to happen. It is the certainty that what we hope for is waiting for us, even though we cannot see it up ahead. Hebrews 11:1 NIV

Heavenly Father,

I thank you for the gift of faith. And I thank you that the quality of this gift is of the highest caliber, for it is the faith of the Son of God, who loves me and gave his life for me.

Help me, Lord, to choose to use my faith in every area of my life. Help me to use my faith as I study and prepare for classes and tests, as I look for a part-time job, or a place to live.

Remind me, Lord, that faith is stimulated and activated by the Word of God. Help me to allow time each day to read your Word. Give me that little inner nudge that reminds me to pray about the things that concern me rather than worry about them.

Help me, Lord, as I grow in knowledge and wisdom and practical application of my chosen field of study, to also grow in the knowledge and practical application of faith.

amen

Chapter Twelve

Balancing Life's Demands

A Personal Checkup

12

Balancing Life's Demands

A checkup is beneficial in any realm of life. We go to the doctor for a physical checkup. We take our car to a mechanic for a checkup. However, when it comes to a personal checkup, each of us must make our own evaluation.

Before you begin your personal checkup, as outlined in this chapter, consider the following three statements, for they are basic to any honest self-estimate.

Consult the architect if you desire to understand the design and function of that which he created.

God is the architect of the human race. He created us according to a specific design and for a specific function. We experience dysfunction in any area of life where we do not operate according to the intended design.

The patterns and habits you develop today are the ones you live with tomorrow.

Habits can be either productive or destructive. Productive patterns help us to grow; they help us in relationships; they help us take care of our bodies; they help us take care of our finances. Good habits produce continuing benefits. Destructive habits drain us and lower our quality of life.

Life is a product of the choices you make, so make right choices.

As you work through this chapter, you can do a personal checkup and evaluate the habits and patterns you have formed.

Checking up . . . . . Spiritually

"Whom have I in heaven but You? And there is none upon earth that I desire besides You. My flesh and heart fail; but God is the strength of my heart and my portion forever." Psalm 73:25, 26

Self-estimate: How am I doing spiritually?

1	2	3	4	5	6	7	8	9	10
Ritual Activity				Growing Communication					Vital Union

Rate yourself on the chart. Circle the number that best describes where you are spiritually. Is your spirituality non-existent or a ritual activity? Is it something you do, not something you are? Then circle 1, 2 or 3. Are you growing in communication with God? Rate yourself somewhere between 4 and 7. Are you in vital union with God? Do you recognize that life truly is in Jesus and apart from the Lord you can be nothing? Rate yourself from 8 to 10.

What's true about me personally?

I find my love, value, and sense of significance through which of the following:

THINGS	RELATIONSHIPS	GOD
Fashion	Boyfriend	Relationship with Jesus
Body Image	Girlfriend	Yielding to God's Spirit
Car I Drive	Parents	Doing God's will
Having Power/Money	Relatives	Searching the Scriptures
Being Respected	Friends	Prayer and Reflection
Special Talents/Abilities	Co-workers	Fellowship with Believers

---

A college professor told how he had to re-evaluate the source of his self-worth when he started college. He said that throughout high school his identity was wrapped up in athletics—especially in being a hockey player. He chose a college where he could continue to play hockey. That first semester, however, the athletic department imported several Canadian students for the hockey team. The professor said that while he was a good hockey player, he could not compete with the Canadians. He didn't make the team and had to do some soul-searching concerning his identity. He came to realize that his sense of identity and self worth was tied to his performance and the way other people evaluated him.

When you walk out into your world everyday, do you start by saying, "I'm not sure who I am. But I hope that things and people come together for me today so I can feel loved and valued"? You don't have to put yourself on the line every day like that. You have a choice.

Now, at the start of your college career, is a good time to do some soul-searching. Is your sense of love, value and significance rooted more in things or relationships than in God? Are you looking for somebody else to come through for you and tell you who you are? If you don't ultimately look to the Lord for a sense of who you are, you will manipulate either things or people to find out who you are.

Thoughts to consider

What you fear becomes your god, and what you fear you revolve your life around.

Do you fear the rejection of your peer group? Are you afraid that you won't fit? Then your life will revolve around trying to fit and being affirmed.

If you're afraid you won't be a success, your life will revolve around attempting to be a success. If you're afraid of not being in a relationship, you'll revolve your life around being in a relationship. The list of things we can fear, and consequently revolve our lives around, is endless. For this reason God tells us to fear Him. If we know that we cannot make it without God, our lives will revolve around Him. God invites us to find fullness and abundance and peace with Him through faith in Jesus Christ.

*Through faith in Jesus each of us finds unmerited favor,
love, value and significance.*

*Without peace with God, we try to find love and significance through manipulating things and relationships to meet the hunger of our hearts—
a hunger only God Himself can meet.*

Resources for growth

Chapel
Bible study
Local church involvement
Personal prayer time
Daily devotions
Read Christian books and magazines

Action Point

What will I personally act on to nurture this area of my life?

_____

_____

_____

_____

Checking up . . . . . . Relationships

"For the Father Himself loves you, because you have loved Me, and have believed that I came forth from God." John 16:27

Self-estimate: How am I doing in relationships?

1	2	3	4	5	6	7	8	9	10

Withdrawn & Shutdown   Reaching Out   Ongoing conflict resolution, commitment, and joy

In any relationship, you start with knowing who you are. If you don't know who you are, you will try to manipulate the person in the relationship with you to meet your needs.

On the chart above check how you are doing in relationships. Are you withdrawn and shut down, afraid of rejection, afraid to risk involvement? Are you actively reaching out to other people? Rate yourself. The pinnacle in relationships is to have ongoing conflict resolution, because conflict is normal for any relationship.

What's true about me personally?

Check the statements that apply.

I feel alone.

I feel guilty about some relationships.

I'm afraid of new relationships.

I love to give to others.

I withdraw from social situations.

I enjoy meeting others' needs.

I worry all the time about my friends.

I hold a lot of bitterness towards others.

I have a short fuse with others.

I know I'm loved.

I know who I am.

I feel special to others.

I feel depressed about relationships.

Thoughts to Consider

Healthy relationships maintain an upward look. Understanding that your deepest needs for love and your sense of significance can only be met in and through your acceptance in Christ enables you to enjoy fullness in relationships. Not knowing who you are in your relationship with God makes it difficult to relate to others.

Two modes of relating.

Giving. Out of personal fullness and self-acceptance, we contribute to the worth and value of others. We also enjoy their contributions to us. We realize that our worth and value are not subject to our performance or the opinion of others.

Manipulating. In relationships based on manipulation, we believe that our personal worth and value are subject to our performance or the opinions of others. Thus, we are compelled to perform in a way that gains us attention and affirmation from others.

Relationships based on manipulation instead of giving are like two ticks with no dog. Ticks attach themselves to a host and draw life from that host. People involved in a relationship who don't know who they are or what they have to give, are like two ticks coming together without a dog. They both try to get the other to respond and meet their need.

Resources for growth	Action Point
Campus spiritual life events	What will I personally act on to bring health to this area of my life?
Campus Bible Study Groups	
Read books on healthy relationships	
Support from close friends	_____
Support groups (community & church)	_____
Personal counseling	_____
Seminars/Conferences on relationships	_____

Checking Up . . . . . Physically

"Or do you not know that your body is the temple of the Holy Spirit, who is in you, whom you have from God, and you are not your own? For you were bought at a price; therefore honor God in your body....." I Corinthians 6:19,20

Self Estimate: How am I doing in taking care of my body?

1	2	3	4	5	6	7	8	9	10
Abusing				Maintaining			Following wellness plan		

What's true about me personally?

I enjoy activities that re-create me.
I understand and practice proper nutrition.
I'm depressed about my appearance.
I exercise weekly and regularly.
I quit exercising routinely.
I have ongoing physical ailments.

I may have a substance abuse problem.
I feel stressed.
I don't sleep regularly.
I never seem to rest.
I'm sexually active.
I feel great!

Thoughts to consider

Lifestyle wellness is a marathon, not a hundred yard dash.
Strive for a balance in nutrition, exercise, work, rest, and recreation.

Students who experience great stress and have difficulty concentrating often find that the source of their problem is physiological. They aren't eating well-balanced regular meals, getting enough sleep, or getting away from study and work. We need to be involved in activities that are expressions of who we are—that are re-creative to us. This is more than recreation; it is special activity that we enjoy.

Resources for growth

Campus Health Center
Personal Physician
Intamural Sports
Personal Fitness Plan
Health Clubs\Gyms
Wellness Literature
Student Resource Center
Health Fairs\Mall Displays

Action Point

What will I personally act on to develop this area of my life?

Nutritional goals _____

Exercise goals _____

Re-creative activities _____

Scheduled rest _____

Checking up . . . . . Psychologically

"We demolish arguments and every pretension that sets itself up against the knowledge of God, and we take captive every thought to make it obedient to Christ." II Corinthians 10:5 (NIV)

Self Estimate: What's my outlook on life?

1	2	3	4	5	6	7	8	9	10

I'm super stressed   I'm keeping up with life   I'm loving life

---

What's true about me personally?

I'm always anxious.

I feel one decision away from failure.

I feel at peace with God and man.

I feel drained.

I'm overwhelmed.

I'm excited about life.

I love life's challenges.

I let my anger rage because I'm frustrated

I'm depressed.

Thoughts to consider.

A goal and a desire are different.
Understanding that difference and its application
will allow for maximum mental health.

GOAL: Something that does not involve the cooperation of others. I assume responsibility for its completion, and I can always achieve it if I work at it.

DESIRE: Something I want, but I can't obtain without the cooperation of others. I can not assume total responsibility for this because it is beyond my control.

The number one rule for good mental health: Never allow something that is actually a desire to become your goal.

For example, a person wants to have a beautiful marriage. That is a desire not a goal, because it involves the cooperation of another person. The person who ties his identity into wanting a beautiful marriage will put pressure on the marriage partner to be what he wants. He does that so he will feel good and his pain level will go down. That person is a manipulator. On the other hand, that same person could enter marriage with a goal to be the best husband possible. That is achievable, regardless of how the marriage partner responds.

Stress builds when people take responsibility for something they cannot control. To derive personal worth and value from the completion of activities that involve the cooperation of another person is not wise.

For example: It's good to set goals academically, but it is not good to tie your self-worth to achieving that goal. To do that is to set yourself up for maximum stress and depression. Be realistic.

Yes, you should study hard and do your best. If your best brings you a 4.0, that is great. But if your best brings you a 3.2, that is also great. You do have limits, and getting that 4.0 is not just up to you; your classroom performance is evaluated by another person.

Never tie your worth and /or value into something you cannot control.

Take a look at the stresses in your life. Ask yourself if you are attaching your worth and value to something you can't control? Part of being psychologically healthy is to define your life. One way to do this is to make a list daily. Above one column write "goal—what I can be responsible for." Above the other write "desire—what involves the cooperation of others." Define these areas and realize that the ones that involve the cooperation of others are areas in which you must trust the Lord, pray, and wait. The goals, however, are your sole responsibility and you can achieve them through concentrated effort.

Resources for growth

The Student Resource Center
Personal study and reflection
Health Center
Campus Spiritual Life Support Groups

Action Point

What areas of my life have I taken 100% responsibility for happening, but in reality they involve the cooperation of others?

_____

_____

_____

_____

Checking up . . . . . . Financially

"Let no debt remain outstanding, except the continuing debt to love one another, for he who loves his fellow man has fulfilled the law." Romans 13:8 (NIV)

Self Estimate: What is my financial condition?

1	2	3	4	5	6	7	8	9	10

I'm out of control   I feel pressure but it's manageable   I keep a balanced budget

---

What's true about me personally?

I don't know where my money goes.
I am maxed out on credit cards.
I'm afraid to assess where I am.
I understand my income and outgo.
I keep good financial records.

I'm anxious over finances.
I'm content where I am.
I binge spend.
I need a personal budget.

Thoughts to consider

The following concepts can help you to understand where you are financially and help you achieve financial peace of mind.

1. Determine current income or allocation and outgo. Whether your money comes from a job or a loan or your parents, that is your allocation.

2. Formulate a budget based upon allocation and stick to it.

3. Develop convictions on what is manageable debt. (How much do I want to borrow? How much do I want to be in debt when I get out of school?) Fill out the worksheet on the next page, and assess where you are financially. Then come up with a monthly budget and stick to it as much as possible.

Monthly Income and Expenses

Income Per Month

Salary _____
Interest _____
Dividends _____
Notes _____
Rents _____

Total Gross Income _____

Less

1. Offerings _____

2. Tax _____

Net spendable income _____

3. Housing

Mortgage/rent _____
Insurance _____
Taxes _____
Electricity _____
Gas _____
Water _____
Telephone _____
Maintenance _____
Other

4. Food _____

5. Automobile(s)

Payments _____
Gas & Oil _____
Insurance _____
Taxes _____
Main/Repair/Replace _____

6. Insurance

Life _____
Medical _____
Other _____

7. Debts

Credit cards _____
Loans & Notes _____
Other _____

8. Entertainment & Recreation

Eating out _____
Trips _____
Baby sitters _____
Activities _____
Vacation _____
Other _____

9. Clothing _____

10. Savings _____

11. Medical Expenses _____

Doctor _____
Dentist _____
Medication _____

12. Miscellaneous

Toiletries _____
Beauty/Barber _____
Laundry _____
Allowances _____
Subscriptions _____
Gifts/Christmas _____
Special Ed. _____
Cash _____
Other _____

Total expenses _____

Income vs. expense _____

Net spendable income _____

Less expenses _____

Checking up . . . . . Academically

"The heart of the discerning acquires knowledge; the ears of the wise seek it out."
Proverbs 18:15 (NIV)

Self Estimate: How am I doing in my classes?

| 1 | 2 | 3 | 4 | 5 | 6 | 7 | 8 | 9 | 10 |

I'm behind
and avoiding them

I'm meeting minimum
expectations

I'm meeting the challenge
and enjoying learning.

What's true about me personally?

I know my academic strengths
and weaknesses.
I'm utilizing campus resources
to assist me.
I have a routine study plan.
I'm attending all classes.

I take good notes.
I utilize study groups.
I participate in class.
I am getting to know my professors.
I ask questions when I'm confused.

Thoughts to consider

Are your classes a challenge or a threat? Classes should be challenging. You should
be saying, "There's more to this than just trying to get an *A*, I'm going to use this
someday."

Are you gaining ground or losing it? Through implementation of the basic study skills
listed above, you can reclaim lost ground, increase academic confidence, and press on
in developing good habits that will help insure academic success.

Resources for growth

Professors
Academic deans
Tutoring programs
Study groups
Study skills elective
Library

Action Point.

What action do I need to take towards
greater academic success?

_____

_____

_____

_____

Checking up . . . . . Vocationally

"Whatever you do, work at it with all your heart, as working for the Lord, not for men." Colossians 3:23 (NIV)

Play to an audience of one. The Lord is the conductor. Do your work unto Him and do it with all your heart and with all your ability.

Self-estimate: How am I doing in developing my vocational plans?

1	2	3	4	5	6	7	8	9	10

I will fall into the right job/major.

I'm investigating my interests, abilities, and major/job options.

I know my personality/skills and the best place to express them.

What's true about me personally?

I don't know what I want to do vocationally.

I don't know what I'm interested in.

I know what skills I have and those I desire to develop.

I think I've chosen the wrong major.

I'm excited about a specific occupation.

I need to explore my occupational options.

I'm anxious about choosing a major.

I know where I'm going in my vocational preparation.

Thoughts to consider

Relating classroom study with an overall vocational goal enhances academic motivation.

Are you a "terminal thinker," or a "relational thinker?"

Terminal thinkers are those who think in a dead end. "I'm going to class. I'm going to get an *A* because that's what I'm supposed to do." They fail to relate what they are learning to anything in life that is practical, or to anything that motivates or impassions them.

Relational thinkers take what they are doing in class and relate it to their lives. "I'm doing well in Chemistry and Biology because someday I want to be a doctor." Or, "I'm doing well in Pre-law classes because I want to be an attorney."

Take AIM on your future.

Assess your aptitudes, interests and skills. Consider your motivations and your desired life goals.

Investigate potentially satisfying jobs. What type of a career will be satisfying to you? What are the minimum entry level requirements, the nature of the work performed, and the entry salary levels?

Market yourself. This includes resume development, proposal development, interview skills and learning how to put together a job market.

The following are suggested components of a comprehensive career assessment and development plan:

Assess

Interests
Aptitudes
Motivation
Desired lifestyle
Life goals
Skills

Investigate

Potential satisfying jobs
Minimum entry level
    requirements
Nature of work
    performed
Entry salary levels
Occupational future

Market

Develop job hunting
    strategy
Define job openings
Develop resume/proposal
Develop interviewing
    skills

Thoughts to consider.

A job does not always go to the person who is best qualified,
but often to the person who knows the most about how to get hired.

Resources for Growth

Student Resource Center

Literature on career development

References in library on careers

Action Point

What will I personally act on to develop this area of my life?

_____

_____

_____

_____

Balancing life's demands is a challenge. It is easy to get caught up in one or two areas and neglect others that are equally important. To stay in balance, it helps to think of each of the areas of life—spiritual, relationships, physical, psychological, financial, academic, and vocation—as slices of a pie. Some slices of the "Pie of Life" are big and some are small. Also, the size of the slices will vary at different points in life. The key to balancing life's demands is to keep all the slices in a round.

For example, you might give four hours to work, five hours to school, and only fifteen minutes to a daily devotion and prayer time. But keep all the slices in there. Don't leave out a slice just because it is small. It's true that you can ignore slices of the pie, like not getting enough sleep or exercise, and seem to get by for a while, but sooner or later it catches up with you. The laws of sowing and reaping are universal principles.

✔ You reap what you sow.

✔ You reap more than you sow.

✔ You reap in a different season.

First, you reap what you sow. If you plant corn, you reap corn. If you plant discipline, you reap the benefits of discipline. If you take care of your body, you reap physical and psychological well-being. If you handle your studies correctly, and prepare academically and vocationally, you are planting good seeds, and you will reap good results.

Second, you reap more than you sow. One seed of corn planted in good soil can yield back several full ears of corn.

Third, you reap in a different season. If you plant seeds of corn, you will reap ears of corn. But it doesn't happen overnight. Some people try planting good seeds of self-discipline, regular study times, proper rest and nutrition for a short time and then give up because they do not see immediate results. They fail to consider the third law of sowing and reaping—you reap in a different season.

Neither does it happen overnight when you begin to erode in any of the areas of life. If you can evaluate where you are today in each of these areas, you can start to do something about it. You can stop planting bad seeds and start planting good seeds. If you neglect the care of your body and pay no attention to your finances, you can get by for a while. However, eventually you will reap what you have planted, and you will reap more of it.

Are you willing to take a good look at your life? to evaluate where you are in each of these areas? This type of evaluation is like looking into a mirror and honestly writing down what you see. The challenge is—what will you do with this evaluation? Are you willing to make the necessary changes—start planting the good seeds that will eventually bring you the results you desire? It's your choice. It's your life.

♥   ♥   ♥

Scripture and Prayer

For in him we live and move and have our being....
Acts 17:28 NIV
He is before all things, and in him all things hold together.
Colossians 1:17 NIV

Heavenly Father,

Suddenly, my life is filled with more demands and responsibilities than ever before. Help me to set priorities and give adequate time and energy to every facet of my life.

Thank you for the information in this chapter. Help me to put it to good use and learn to balance life's demands—whether they be in the classroom, on the job, with friends and family, or with you.

It helps, Lord, to know that you know and understand where I am and all that I face. And I am especially thankful that you have promised to always be with me and help me. So thank you again for holding all the pieces of my life together.

amen

Appendix

Student Activities, Clubs and Organizations

Activities, Clubs and Organizations

Student activities, clubs and organizations are an important part of college life. The history behind these kinds of student activities dates back to the 1800's.

Back then there was no interaction between the professors and the students during class. The students just sat and took notes while the professors lectured. Eventually the students decided that they needed to expand their minds and escape from the humdrum of the curriculum, so they started debate teams. Then they formed intramural sport programs and academic clubs.

Benefits

The benefits of being in an activity, a club, or an organization are many. First, you meet new people and have the opportunity to make a lot of new friends and develop friendships. You might even meet someone you would like to date.

Benefits of being involved in intramurals are exercise and stress relief as well as team camaraderie. Normally, the intramural sports programs are a reflection of your intercollegiate athletics. Depending on the school, you could choose basketball, baseball, volleyball, golf, and other sports.

Development of leadership skills is an important benefit of being involved in a club or organization. Many of you may think that you don't have time to get involved in a club or organization, but think about this: Four years from now when you graduate, what will be the difference between you and the person sitting next to you? You'll both have diplomas, but a lot of people out there are going to have diplomas. The experience and skills you acquire from participating in a club or organization can give you the edge when it comes to finding employment.

Skills you can gain through involvement in clubs, organizations and student activities include:

- ✔ motivational techniques
- ✔ conflict resolution
- ✔ communication skills
- ✔ learn to facilitate meetings
- ✔ learn to delegate responsibility
- ✔ learn to manage people and manage money
- ✔ acquire decision making skills
- ✔ problem solving
- ✔ project management
- ✔ planning and organization
- ✔ volunteer recruitment.

Picture yourself sitting in front of a prospective employer after you graduate and he says, "Tell me what kind of experience you have."

You could answer, "I was a member of the student accounting club. I was the president of it one year." And even if you weren't an officer in the club, you will have gained experience in various areas.

College is the perfect environment to get involved in clubs and organizations. You have a lot of support, and you can take some risks without having a job on the line. It's much easier to try out your communication skills in the college environment of a club than out there in the job market.

In clubs you have the support of your peers and your advisors. The advisors of your clubs and organizations are there to help you, to guide you, and if you do fall, to help you get back up and get going again. You also have the help of administrators. Most universities and colleges do not allow just any club or organization to take place on campus. It has to benefit the student body as a whole. I encourage you to explore the possibilities and get involved with different clubs and organizations. You should be able to find everything from academics to athletics to foreign languages.

Another benefit of being involved in student activities is that you will have something to put on your resume when you apply for a job. All of these extra-curricular activities are a definite plus and can help you gain the position you desire after graduation.

Activities, Clubs and Organizations

1. List the activities, clubs and organizations on campus that interest you.

   _____

   _____

   _____

   _____

   _____

   _____

   _____

   _____

2. Now, select one or two that you would like to participate in this semester.

   _____

   _____

   _____

3. Next semester.

   _____

   _____

4. In future years.

   _____

   _____

   _____

   _____

5. Find out when and where the club or activity of your choice meets, and write that information below. Also, make a notation on your time management planner.

_____

_____

_____

_____

_____

_____

♥   ♥   ♥

Scripture and Prayer

There is a time for everything, and a season for every activity under heaven. Ecclesiastes 3:1 NIV

Heavenly Father,

I thank you for the opportunity to be a part of campus clubs and organizations. Help me to select at least one activity that I will enjoy and that I can contribute to. Thank you for this opportunity to relate to others in a positive way, and to acquire and practice techniques and skills that will help me in the future.

amen

Mentors: Partners For Success

Sherri Willborn

Mentors

Success is never attained alone. Someone, or in most cases, many someones, have stood beside us, nudged us along, criticized us a bit, and praised us a lot! They sense our pain before it ever pierces our hearts. They celebrate with us in small victories, and keep us hopeful for our future. These special people become our shadows, giving us an image to follow in the brightness of our days, and a comfort in spirit when we cannot see them in the dark circumstances that will assuredly face us. They are our MENTORS.

As a college student you **will** have a mentor. It may be through a formal program such as University 101. Or you may meet someone who will unexpectedly become a treasured confidante.

The setting of this encounter could be quite bizarre.

Take for instance, the day several years ago when I met the man who changed the course of my college destiny. No, it wasn't Mr. Right, nor was it the night-shift janitor. It was the Dean of Students who was partaking of a gourmet entree in the cafeteria. It was his custom to eat lunch with the students when his schedule allowed.

On this particular day, he sat down at my table. We were already acquainted and had passed each other in the hallways several times. He, however, decided to open a conversation. As I recall, he was addressing a stress-related topic such as "midterm exams." He could see the agony in my face, the dark shadows under my eyes expressing an all-night cram session in the dorms. He could see the effects of rows of empty Diet Coke cans whose contents had been used as dangerous doses of caffeine.

In a humorous manner, the Dean tried desperately to cheer me up. When he noticed little success, he pulled out a straw and with an invisible Bic lighter, lit the straw and started to smoke it!

Try to envision a very proper, highly respected administrative figure smoking a pack of straws! No nicotine, no black lungs, no warning from the Surgeon General. It was hysterical! I followed suit, and within moments everyone at our table had "lit up." We laughed until tears rolled down our cheeks.

On several occasions throughout that semester we were caught in public places "smoking straws," to release tension. However, an important and marvelous relationship blossomed. The Dean and I became friends, to the point that he helped me through some difficult times in determining an academic major, surviving the pitfalls of dating, and teaching me how to prioritize my responsibilities.

I owe a great deal to this man. Though our paths rarely cross anymore, if I should see him again, we would certainly share a straw and a story.

Because of that positive relationship, I find it a great privilege to be a mentor for University Success. As a mentor, I see the journey that lies before you. I understand the fears of being in an unknown college environment. I sympathize with your financial strain and the endless questions of, "How will I pay for next semester?" I feel the pressure of final exams. I sense the curiosity of the job market. I loathe the sting of your heartbreak. I celebrate the fun of your new friends. Those are the characteristics of any mentor. Put simply, your mentor will care about **you.**

Your mentor will participate with you in several of the University Success classes, and may have tiny pearls of wisdom to share. The greatest joy for your mentor, though, will be in hearing your discoveries and insights from lectures, laboratory experiences, and hallway encounters.

Take advantage of the resources a mentor provides. Many of them are professors or staff professionals who know the "right people for the right time." They may have knowledge in academic advising, financial aid, campus activities, career options, and counseling.

Mentors are as useful as you allow them to be. Maybe what you need is a stress break. One of my traditions as a mentor is to host "a chocolate chip cookie dough party" each semester. My "mentees" and I make the dough and eat it RAW. It's delicious and potent enough to cure what ails you at the time!

Whether you are a freshman with no college experience, a transfer student, or an adult returning student with an abundance of life experience, your mentor will be available to walk the journey with you.

My hope and prayer is that you will discover a definition of success that is meaningful for you. You never have to walk alone, our God is the greatest example of a mentor. He cares very deeply for you. And you will discover that He has appointed people to interrupt you in the hallway and share your vision of success. Remember, if it happens to be me, we will light a straw and share a story.

Mentors

You can use this form to schedule appointments with your mentors in various classes. Space is also provided for you to jot down questions you may want to ask when you meet with them.

Class_____   Name of Mentor_____
Appointments   Questions

_____

_____

_____

_____

_____

Class_____   Name of Mentor_____
Appointments   Questions

_____

_____

_____

_____

_____

Class_____   Name of Mentor_____
Appointments   Questions

_____

_____

_____

_____

_____

Class_____   Name of Mentor_____
Appointments   Questions

_____

_____

_____

_____

_____

Class_____   Name of Mentor_____
Appointments   Questions

_____

_____

_____

_____

_____

♥ ♥ ♥

Scripture and Prayer

Pay attention and listen to the sayings of the wise…Apply your heart to what I teach, for it is pleasing when you keep them in your heart and have all of them ready on your lips.
Proverbs 22:17 NIV
*Make plans by seeking advice….*Proverbs 20:18 NIV

Heavenly Father,

I thank you for the people who have experienced what I am going through right now. I thank you that so many of them are willing to share the insights they have gained.

Help me to see my need of help from others and to avail myself of that provision, and thus add another dimension to my college experience.

amen

Index